WOMEN'S HEALTH, PUBLIC POLICY AND COMMUNITY ACTION

Women's Health, Public Policy and Community Action

Edited by
SWAPNA MUKHOPADHYAY

MANOHAR
1998

First published 1998

© Institute of Social Studies Trust, 1998

All rights reserved. No part of this publication may be reproduced or transmitted, in any form or by any means, without prior permission of the editor and the publisher

ISBN 81-7304-103-2

Published by
Ajay Kumar Jain for
Manohar Publishers & Distributors
2/6 Ansari Road, Daryaganj
New Delhi 110002

Printed at
Rajkamal Electric Press
B 35/9 G T Karnal Road Indl Area
Delhi 110033

Acknowledgements

This is a compendium of revised versions of papers presented in a National Seminar on Women's Health and Reproduction organized by the Institute of Social Studies Trust, New Delhi in November 1995 as part of a project titled 'Poverty, Gender Inequality and Reproductive Choice' then under way at ISST. The papers arranged in four sections situate women's health issues within the primary health scenario in India.

We are grateful to the John D. and Catherine T. MacArthur Foundation for sponsoring the study and the seminar. We are also very grateful to all the paper writers and participants in the seminar whose combined expertise and experience made it a very lively and worthwhile exercise. The editorial introduction on the centrality of community involvement and gender sensitivity in the design and implementation of public policy in matters concerning women's health provides the basic framework within which the individual papers are situated. The volume brings together a wealth of information and insights from leading experts in reproductive and community health and NGO activists, which we hope will be of value to policy planners and health professionals involved in the field of women's reproductive health within the broad parameters of primary health care in the country.

NEW DELHI   SWAPNA MUKHOPADHYAY
23 March 1997

Contents

Acknowledgements 5
List of Abbreviations 9
Introduction
   Swapna Mukhopadhyay 11

I. MACRO SCENARIO ON HEALTH

Planning for Women's Health: The Indian Experience
   Krishna Soman 23
Health Sector Financing in the Context of Women's Health
   Ravi Duggal 37
Gender Equality and Political Participation: Implications for Good Health
   A.K. Shiva Kumar 53

II. MICRO STUDIES ON GENDER AND REPRODUCTION

Poverty, Gender Inequality and Reproductive Choice: Some Findings from a Household Survey in U.P.
   Swapna Mukhopadhyay, Praachi Tewari Gandhi and R. Savithri 71
The Contours of Reproductive Choice for Poor Women: Findings from a Micro Survey
   Swapna Mukhopadhyay and Surekha Garimella 98

III. NGO INITIATIVES IN HEALTH CARE

Women in Panchayati Raj: Implications for Health for All
   N.H. Antia and Nerges Mistry 125
Reaching Women Through Children at CINI
   S.N. Chaudhuri 131

Rural Women's Social Education Centre, Chengalpattu:
Case Study of a Grassroots Organization Working for
Health Promotion Through Women's Empowerment
T.K. Sundari Ravindran 138

IV. POLICY ISSUES

India's Augean Stables: The Unfinished Health Agenda
Mohan Rao 151

Seminar Proceedings 167

Seminar Agenda 184

Contributors 188

Index 189

List of Abbreviations

AIDS	Acquired Immuno Deficiency Syndrome
ANC	Ante Natal Care
ANM	Auxiliary Nurse Midwife
CEHAT	Centre for Enquiry Into Health and Allied Themes
CHC	Community Health Centre
CHV	Community Health Volunteer
CINI	Child In Need Institute
CSSM	Child Survival and Safe Motherhood
FRCH	The Foundation for Research in Community Health
GDP	Gross Domestic Product
GOBI	Growth Monitoring, Oral Rehydration, Breast Feeding and Immunization
GOI	Government of India
ICDS	Integrated Child Development Services
ICMR	Indian Council of Medical Research
ICPD	International Conference on Population and Development
ICSSR	Indian Council of Social Science Research
IIPS	International Institute for Population Sciences
IUCD	Intra Uterine Contraceptive Device
LHW	Lady Health Worker
MCH	Maternal and Child Health
MMR	Maternal Mortality Rate
MNP	Minimum Needs Programme
MPW	Multi-Purpose Worker
NACO	National AIDS Control Organization
NAEP	National Adult Education Programme
NCAER	National Council of Applied Economic Research
NFHS	National Family Health Survey
NGO	Non-Governmental Organization
NIHFW	National Institute of Health and Family Welfare
NIPFP	National Institute of Public Finance and Policy
NRC	Nutrition Rehabilitation Centre
NSSO	National Sample Survey Organization
NTP	National Tuberculosis Programme

ORT	Oral Rehydration Therapy
PHC	Primary Health Centre
PHN	Public Health Nurse
PNC	Post Natal Care
RTI	Reproductive Tract Infection
RUWSEC	Rural Women's Social Education Centre
SIDA	Swedish International Development Cooperative Agency
SRS	Sample Registration System
STD	Sexually Transmitted Diseases
UIP	Universal Immunization Programme
UNICEF	United Nations Children's Educational Fund
VHW	Village Health Worker
WHO	World Health Organization

Introduction

SWAPNA MUKHOPADHYAY

CAIRO ICPD: THE WATERSHED

Official recognition of women's health needs in India has been singularly focused on women's child-bearing functions. This explains why women's health has been inexorably tied up with the government's family planning programme. The International Conference on Population and Development (ICPD), held in Cairo in September 1994, marked a watershed in the rhetoric if not the substantive content of population policy debates the world over. Its implications have been very pronounced for Third World countries, including India. From target-oriented, demographically driven macro-level fertility control programmes, attention has shifted to concerns of the individual woman—her rights over her body, her health status and her choice in reproductive matters. In the aftermath of the deliberations before, during and after the Conference, the target- and incentive-driven family planning programme in India has been sought to be replaced with a target-free, reproductive-health approach. The reoriented family planning programme has been operative since April 1996. Whether or not it signals a paradigmatic shift in official policy and thinking, time alone will tell.

The Cairo document came in the wake of intense negotiations between a wide range of actors of diverse political and ideological persuasions. But much as the international feminist lobby may rejoice in the outcome of the Conference in the shape of the Plan of Action, and its overtly feminist language and orientation, there is little doubt that the convergence would not have taken place if a myriad of actors, including the US State Department, had not decided to put the full weight of their support behind the pro-abortionist, safe-motherhood platform. It is a different matter that the explicit nature of the support from the Clinton administration may have been activated by the domestic political exigency of taking a stand against the pro-natalist, anti-abortionist stance of the erstwhile Republican administration, or that the final outcome got tempered by resistance from the rather unlikely alliance of the Holy See with Islamic fundamentalist forces in favour of traditional family values and the rights of the unborn.

The traditional population lobby in India, which has generally been spurred by the alarmist vision of a world bursting at the seams with uncontrolled population explosion in Third World countries, had for some time been coming round to the view that targeted population control programmes have not merely failed to deliver the goods even in terms of controlling fertility, but they would continue to do so unless they are substantially revised in favour of greater sensitivity to people's needs and priorities. The feminist lobby had already been advocating a gender-sensitive approach to population and developmental issues. The Women's Health Movement had, within the span of a decade, coalesced into a formidable pressure group, with protagonists from all over the world. Feminist scholars, activists and NGOs working in the area of women's health in India, who have long been protesting against the hierarchical and insensitive nature of the official family planning programme, found a strong base within the international movement for a pro-woman, reproductive-health approach. All these factors combined to generate the final convergence of positions that emerged as a consensus document at the end of the Conference.

The new paradigm of reproductive health that seeks to replace the fertility control approach of the traditional population lobby, places the individual woman—her reproductive rights, choice and health—at the central core of concerns. The reproductive health approach emphasizes the agency of people themselves to reproduce and regulate their fertility. It ensures safe pregnancy and childbirth as well as healthy survival of mother and child. It also incorporates the need for the involvement of both partners in the freedom to have sexual relations without the fear of disease or unwanted pregnancies (Fatallah 1988; Pachauri 1995).

OFFICIAL POLICY ON WOMEN'S HEALTH

Women's health *per se* has never held the centre stage in official thinking and policy design in India, except in the limited context of women's child-bearing functions. The alarmingly high levels of maternal mortality and morbidity cited in the reports of the Bhore Committee and a number of other committees appointed by the government around the time of independence prompted the government to subject maternal and child health to separate programmatic action under the five-year plans. In terms of the percentage of budget allocation for health, however, MCH has been a very insignificant component. Considering that health and family welfare together has barely ever exceeded 3 per cent of total budget allocations at the Centre, the paucity of financial resources on MCH services becomes obvious. Krishna Soman's paper in this volume traces the history of the MCH programme in the context of health planning for women in India.

India was the first country to launch a country-wide family planning programme with the objective of reducing the rate of population growth in the aggregate. With the exception of the Emergency years of 1975-7, women have been the primary targets of official family planning drives. Centrally conceived and centrally administered, the official family planning programme has been target-driven and non-participatory by design, and has been known to have led to coercive practices such as mass sterilizations with little attention to provision of requisite medical advice or ensuring the delivery of necessary health services to the clients.

The absence of sensitivity in the design and implementation of the official family planning programme has been highlighted by a wide range of critics. Female sterilization has been by far the most frequently used method of contraception in India, with little concern for the women's pre-operation health status or for post-operative care. Invasive contraceptive technology has been sought to be promoted without sufficient information or precaution regarding after-effects. Incentives have been announced for acceptors and field-level staff for pre-assigned sterilization targets. The idea has been that such covertly coercive measures would bring down the aggregate rate of growth of population (Sen 1995). However, apart from the ethical issue of whether State coercion is justifiable in an area of one's life as personal as reproductive behaviour, coercive measures often turn out to be much less effective than hoped. Older women who have already reached their desired family size may opt for tubectomy. Targets would be reached and monetary incentives taken but the impact on the rate of population growth may be negligible. In the process, women's health concerns would be side-tracked in the urgency of reaching official contraceptive targets.

There has also been a pervasive lack of understanding regarding the multifarious pressures throughout the lives of women especially from poor households, that militate against their chances of leading a healthy life. Poverty, general lack of resources, information and infrastructure, are one set of factors that affects both sexes. The other relates to widespread gender discrimination even in the provision of basic needs that disadvantages women in particular. Women much more than men have a raw deal within each socio-economic stratum because they are discriminated against right from birth. Poor women suffer the most because household resources are inadequate to start with. Unequal access to nutrition, health care and education, early marriage, low autonomy in most areas of operation, the social responsibility for bearing and rearing of children, maintaining the household and ensuring family survival, combine with a heavy workload to generate a state of endemic anaemia and poor health for the majority. The paper by Mukhopadhyay, Tewari Gandhi and Savithri brings out the nature of interlinkages between poverty, gender discrimination and fertility behaviour of poor rural women from a sample survey of 1,078 households in five districts of the state of Uttar Pradesh. Patriarchal values are so entrenched that the majority of women can barely assert themselves against forced sex within marriage and are in no position to handle unwanted pregnancies safely and in free conscience. The paper by Mukhopadhyay and Garimella seeks to delve into the complexities and inner tensions associated with sex and reproduction within marriage by charting out the inconsistencies in the responses of women and men on issues such as unwanted pregnancies, abortion and women's reproductive autonomy from a sample survey of households in rural Kumaon and urban Delhi. A hierarchically structured official programme that fails to integrate such basic parameters of the women's life situation in its design and implementation processes is unlikely to deliver the goods.

REPRODUCTIVE HEALTH APPROACH: THE NEW PARADIGM

As a result of concerted pressure from the Women's Health Movement and the official commitments made at the ICPD-1994, the Government of India has started a new target-free approach in family welfare from April 1996. A manual has been drawn up at the Ministry of Health and Family Welfare for the benefit of government functionaries who are to implement this approach. There is an increased tolerance at the official level to the idea of moving away from targets and incentives to reduce fertility, to broaden the concept of MCH to that of reproductive and child health (RCH) and to emphasize a client-centred approach. The revamped RCH approach, however, despite the wider focus, is still too narrow. It begins and ends with maternal health, leaving out women outside reproductive age groups, thus ignoring the ground reality that maternal morbidity is to a considerable extent caused by factors carried over from intra-household discrimination against young girls, or that old women's disabilities are often the result of gender discrimination earlier. Also, while acknowledging the need and importance of a client-based approach, the reoriented policy of reproductive and child health still keeps the target population in the shadow. Women nowhere figure in the design, implementation or monitoring of the programme. The policy thus continues to be non-participatory and restrictive.

This is unfortunate, for the central theme—and what many believe is the legacy of the Cairo ICPD—has been to shift attention from the demographically driven goal of controlling aggregate fertility to the concern of the individual woman—her reproductive choice and her rights over her body. The parameters of such choice and the limits of her rights are not context-free. They invoke differing issues and problems under divergent socio-economic and cultural settings. The nature of such parameters needs to be explored if women's choice and rights in reproductive matters in a specific context have to be understood and mapped out.

There is a point of view that the language and the conceptualization of the new approach on women's health and reproductive rights is foreign to both the context and major concerns of women of India. It has been argued that in pinpointing the issues of reproductive health and rights as women's central concern across the world, the varying social contexts of women from different countries with differing life situations have been obliterated in favour of an artificial, meaningless homogeneity (Qadeer 1996). In the process, it is argued, the links between general health and reproductive health, and their links with the socio-economic context, have been blurred.

Whether women's reproductive health should be advocated as a separate programme activity or looked upon as part of the broader area of primary health has been debated in many forums. Protagonists of the former approach claim that if reproductive health is seen in the totality of general health, it will lose the much-needed official support and recognition it has received in recent times. They argue that women's reproductive health needs are so pervasive and so little articulated that unless they get separate and distinct programmatic attention, they are bound to remain neglected. They cite in supportive evidence the strong programmatic support that HIV/AIDS prevention activities and the gender dimensions of the spread of the disease among single-partner married have received in recent times from international agencies.

Those who advocate the holistic approach believe that segregating reproductive health, besides being artificial, is inimical to treating women's health in its totality. By separating reproductive health from the woman's specific life situation and by isolating it from the socio-economic context of her existence, the approach misses out on certain essential linkages that invests it with meaning and content.

The critics also argue that those who single out reproductive health as the central issue of women's health, are oblivious that in a country like India, communicable diseases kill more women even in the reproductive age groups than maternal deaths do. Superimposing a high-profile reproductive health servicing package on the already overburdened MCH programme, they point out, might result in spreading the infrastructure too thin and side-tracking the more urgent need of bringing down maternal mortality rates to more acceptable levels, especially so, since the general health needs of vast sections of the population go largely uncatered to even now. A whole range of issues dealing with financing of the public health sector, allocation and use of financial and other resources within the sector and the impact of structural adjustment programmes on all these factors assume importance in this context. Ravi Duggal's paper in this volume provides the outlines of a comprehensive public health policy addressing a number of these issues.

CAN THE STATE DELIVER THE GOODS?

State responsibility in India in health delivery has always had a pronounced focus on curative rather than preventive care, and has always had a strong urban bias, even as primary health care in the country has still a long way to go in terms of quality and coverage, and the vast majority of Indians still live in rural areas. Mohan Rao's paper in this volume provides a critical review of health policy in the country for the last two decades. The primary health care network in the country, consisting of community health workers, village health workers, *anganwadi* workers, primary health centres and sub-centres, auxiliary nurse midwives, male multipurpose workers and PHC doctors, has failed to cater to the health needs of the rural populace. Absence of accountability, inefficient planning and inadequate resources have rendered PHCs and sub-centres built across country in many ways non-functional; they often lack doctors and medicines. Poor infrastructure across rural India compounds the people's hardships. Hierarchically designed programmes, some of them targeted to specific population groups, have jostled for space and prominence at the ground level, on account of poor synchronization and planning. Often lower level functionaries like the ANMs and the *anganwadi* workers have had to bear the brunt of official experimentation, increasing their work burden on already overloaded schedules without any additional infrastructural support. Given the enormity of the unfinished health agenda and the dismal record of official performance in the area of both community health in general and women's health in particular, one could legitimately wonder whether the State, with its bloated and entrenched official health hierarchies and its legendary distance from the people, especially the poor, can indeed deliver the goods. More so in the field of RCH intervention, which at present is essentially tentative and incrementalist in nature. Is the State machinery indeed capable of matching the new rhetoric of reproductive health with commensurate action? *The Manual on Target-Free Approach in Family Welfare*, produced by the Ministry of Health and Family Welfare, that attempts to spell out the procedures for planning, monitoring and evaluation of field activities in the target-free era, for example, envisions virtually no involvement of or role for local women in the whole process. Other examples can be cited. The draft National Population Policy prepared by the Ministry in November 1996 recommends, among other things, modifying the service rules in government employment to debar from recruitment or promotion those who had married underage or those having more than two children. Obviously, the inherent coercive inclination in policy planning will take a long time to change. How then to meet the urgent necessity of providing comprehensive health care to the people, especially the poor who cannot afford private medical care? In this context, the work of non-governmental agencies, many of which have a long record of dedicated, innovative community health service, with an emphasis on preventive care and community participation, assumes much significance.

THE NGO EXPERIENCE IN HEALTH CARE

Non-government organizations in India are very heterogeneous in size, character, orientation, commitment and motivation. They may be loosely characterized as private non-profit organizations registered as public trusts or associations which are voluntary associations of people working for the benefit of the poor and vulnerable sections of society. Many of the older NGOs started as charitable organizations, forums for voluntary welfare work, often with a religious overtone. In recent times India has seen a spurt of NGOs, largely of secular persuasion, with a strong focus on people's participation and community empowerment.

In health care delivery, quite a few NGOs have displayed innovativeness and cost-effectiveness. The secret of success of the better NGOs stems from their closeness to the people, resulting in much greater sensitivity of the programmes to the ground realities and flexibility. The three papers by Antia and Mistry, Ravindran and Chaudhuri on NGO experiments in health care highlight this aspect. The five year plan documents have recognized the necessity of bringing about a collaborative arrangement between the official agencies and the NGOs for more efficient delivery of government programmes to the people. Apart perhaps from primary education, no other area needs such tie-ups more than health, especially women's health. Such collaboration should not just be operational with NGOs delivering government programmes on the ground. The official machinery has a long way to go in terms of internalizing the spirit and culture of NGO initiatives both in the design as well as in the implementation strategies. This involves a holistic understanding of health—not simply in terms of treatment of illness but as a function of the overall development of society. The recent 73rd Amendment to the Constitution of India has provided a golden opportunity to translate such ideas through the mediation of the local panchayat structure. Some NGO activities along these lines are already underway (Antia and Mistry's paper in this volume). The salient features of such endeavours include community involvement in the maintenance of overall state of good health and well-being, and the practice of targeting the poorest and most vulnerable sections of society.

The present volume contains papers—revised for publication—presented in a National Seminar on 'Gender, Health and Reproduction', organized by the Institute of Social Studies Trust in November 1995 in New Delhi. The seminar brought together experts—practitioners as well as academics—from the areas of community health, reproductive health and feminist studies. During the four half-day sessions spanning two days, the participants reviewed the macro scenario and findings from some recent micro studies on reproductive health of women in India, examined some of the innovative NGO experiments in the area and collectively analysed the various dimensions of health policy. Together, the papers in this volume hope to provide a backdrop to informed analysis of women's reproductive health issues in the context of public policy as well as community involvement. Short summaries of the papers presented at the seminar and a summary of the discussions are appended at the end of the volume.

REFERENCES

Fatallah, M., 1988. 'Research Needs in Human Reproduction' in E. Diczfalusy, P.D. Griffin and J. Kharlna (eds.), *Research in Human Reproduction. Biennial Report (1986-87)*, Geneva, World Health Organization.

Government of India, 1996. Manual on Target-Free Approach in Family Welfare Programme, Ministry of Health and Family Welfare, New Delhi.

Institute of Social Studies Trust, 1996. Background documents presented at the workshop on 'Reproductive Health Through the Panchayats' (Ongoing project at ISST), 10-12 July, New Delhi.

Mukhopadhyay, Swapna and R. Savithri, 1998. *Poverty, Gender and Reproductive Choice: An Analysis of Linkages*, Manohar, New Delhi.

Pachauri, Saroj, 1995. Defining a Reproductive Health Package for India: A Proposed Framework. Regional Working Paper No. 4, Population Council, New Delhi.

Qadeer, Imrana, 1996. 'Rights and Reproductive Health: A Perspective'. Unpublished paper presented at the Workshop on 'Rights and Reproductive Health in India's Primary Care' organized by the School of Social Sciences, Jawaharlal Nehru University, New Delhi, 4-5 November.

Sen, Amartya K., 1995. *Population Policy: Authoritarianism versus Cooperation*. International Lecture Series on Population Issues, John D. and Catherine T. MacArthur Foundation, New Delhi.

I
Macro Scenario on Health

1
Macro Scenario on Health

Planning for Women's Health: The Indian Experience

Krishna Soman

This paper attempts to explore the nature and implications of planning for women's health in India. It traces the strategies and priorities in planning during and after independence, followed by the evolution of maternal and child health (MCH) programme. It discusses some major implications of planning for women's health, and examines the role of non-governmental organizations (NGOs) in health development in India.

PLANNING AT INDEPENDENCE

In the long history of health provision in India, women's health has been perceived by the planners primarily in the context of motherhood. At independence, there were two important documents, which later influenced the five-year plan documents on health planning. The first report was the recommendations of the National Health and Development Committee (1946), more commonly known as the Bhore Committee. The other was the recommendations of the National Planning Committee, also known as the Sokhey Committee, which was set up in 1938 and whose recommendations were published in 1948.

The Bhore Committee noted that

> the health of the people depends primarily upon the social and environmental conditions under which people live and work, upon security against fear and want, upon nutritional standards, upon educational facilities, and upon facilities for exercise and leisure. ... A nation's health is perhaps the most potent single factor in determining the character and extent of its development and progress and any expenditure of money and effort on improving the national health is a gilt-edged investment yielding immediate and steady returns in increased productive capacity. (GOI 1946, I: 63)

This understanding of people's health, and its importance in improving national productivity, underlay the Bhore Committee's recommendations.

The Sokhey Committee in its turn noted that: 'Mother and child are very largely helpless and dependent; and for their protection the State has therefore to step in' (GOI 1946, IV: 26-8).

Both committees thus gave due attention to mother and child health. The Bhore Committee, concerned about the high incidence of morbidity and mortality among mothers and children, recommended measures directed toward a reduction of these ills by setting a high priority on preventive, promotive and curative care in health development. At independence, maternal mortality rate (MMR) in certain provinces was as high as 12.9 per 1,000 live births and 50 per cent of the maternal deaths were due to puerperal sepsis and anaemia.

The Bhore Committee's recommendations were both long-term (stretching over twenty to forty years) and short-term, spread over two to five-year periods. The committee evolved a three-tier organizational set-up at the district level, and also village-level health committees of five to seven volunteers to help in the activities of the primary health unit. As an immediate measure, the committee recommended a primary health unit serving a population of 20,000 with one woman doctor, four public health nurses (PHN), four midwives and four trained *dais*. There would be four beds at the primary health unit, specially earmarked for maternity cases. Every four such primary health units were to have, in addition, a thirty-bed hospital with a special medical officer for MCH work (GOI 1972-3: 76-8).

The Sokhey Committee, in similar recommendations, urged integrated and State-supported curative and preventive services, which were to be provided by trained health workers for a fixed size of population (GOI 1989: 1-10). Of particular interest was the committee's recognition of women's economic role and concern for their health in relation to the environment at the place of work. For this it recommended 'legal protection of women's labour in factories'. In addition to the Factory Act of 1934 (which regulated the hours of work for women and employment of expectant and nursing mothers), it also recommended that the establishment of creches must be compulsory in factories which employed nursing mothers. Another recommendation was to bring all the provinces under the Maternity Benefit Act. The five year health planning was initiated in India based on the Sokhey Committee's recommendations of integrated preventive, promotive and curative health care for pregnant, lactating and working women and the Bhore committee's recommendations for a three-tier organizational structure for maternal health at the district level. Provision of health services to the entire population was adopted as a directive principle of State policy (Basu 1970).

THE FIVE-YEAR PLANS

Health planning in India has been shaped by the strategies of overall development. Though initially 'maternal health' received an emphasis in the context of national development, its evolution has been influenced by the felt urgency of the planners for family planning and control of communicable diseases. This is reflected in the trends of allocation of funds for and within the health sector. The place given to MCH in the list of priorities has been influenced by the shifts in the strategies of planning. The development of infrastructure for MCH has also been influenced by the policies of 'integration of services'. Even within the MCH, planning tilted more in favour of child health rather than mother's health, till the mid-1970s.

In planning, budget is sanctioned for 'Health and Family Welfare'. Accordingly, budget allocations are divided into Family Welfare and programmes covered by Health (Table 1).

It is seen from Table 1 that, over the five-year plans, investment in Health and Family Welfare has always remained below the recommended proportion (10 per cent) of the total allocation on development. Though investment in health has been higher than in Family Welfare, the gap between the two has been decreasing over time. Also, within the Health and Family Welfare sector, Family Welfare has received a higher priority than other subsectors except water supply and sanitation (Table 2). While resources for critical public health programmes, viz., control of major communicable diseases, were curtailed, efforts were made to integrate these concerns at the periphery through redesignation of uni-purpose workers. Thus while allocations were curtailed, an attempt was made to use the existing infrastructure for catering to multiple needs. Theoretically, the infrastructure was expected to back up multiple services, but in reality, public health programmes were neglected (Qadeer 1995).

The Plan documents do not provide information on the allocation for the specific components within the Plans such as family planning and MCH (GOI 1990: Annexure 12.6, 329). Nevertheless, while tracing the evolution of programmes, it becomes clear that even within MCH, maternal health concerns have been undermined by allocating more services for the children.

STRATEGIES

The health strategies chosen for development in the country have echoed the developments in the international arena. In health, protection of the health of the mother and her children was of utmost importance at the initial stage, in order to build a sound and healthy nation through socio-economic development (GOI 1951, 1956). Since the Third Plan, the idea of population growth in a scenario of limited resources has dominated the health planning process (GOI 1961). The MCH which included maternal health, no longer attracted the priority that the family planning programme did. But the scene changed in the Fourth Plan (GOI 1970), marking a shift towards a broad-based developmental perspective. At the World Population Conference of 1974 in Bucharest, India's health minister raised the slogan, 'Development is the Best Contraceptive'. The change of political power in 1977 following the period of Emergency emphasized 'People's health in people's hands'. A need for community participation was felt by the planners. This also coincided with the strategy of 'Health for All by AD 2000' declared in Alma Ata the same year (ICSSR and ICMR 1981). 'Health for All' was to be achieved through primary health care approach which, among its principles, emphasized community participation and inter-sectoral coordination. This strategy was adopted in the Fifth Plan. The Plan promised minimum public health facilities integrated with family planning and nutrition for the vulnerable groups which included pregnant and lactating mothers (GOI 1980b).

During this Plan period, the National Population Policy of 1976 (GOI 1976) had recognized poverty as the real enemy of development. The Working Group on Population Policy in 1980, however, equated general developmental strategy and population policy as 'two sides of the same coin' (GOI 1980a). Yet again, the Sixth Plan in the early 1980s shifted its emphasis back to limiting the growth of population (GOI 1985).

Though the National Population Policy of 1976 had asserted that 'the process of development is apt to be lopsided unless socio-economic imbalances in the health services are removed speedily', it had accepted 'birth control' as a vital means to the attainment of the goal of 'Health for All, in the shortest possible time' (GOI 1976).

TABLE 1. PATTERN OF INVESTMENT IN 'HEALTH AND FAMILY WELFARE' (ACTUAL)
(RS. IN CRORES)

Plan period		Total Plan Outlay	Health	Family Welfare	Sub Total
First Plan:	1951-6	1,960	65.2	0.1	65.3
		(100)	(3.3)	(-)	(3.3)
Second Plan:	1956-61	4,672.0	140.8	5.0	145.8
		(100)	(3.0)	(0.1)	(3.1)
Third Plan:	1961-6	8,576.5	225.9	24.9	250.8
		(100)	(2.6)	(0.3)	(2.9)
Annual Plans:	1966-9	6,625.4	140.2	70.4	210.6
		(100)	(2.1)	(1.1)	(3.2)
Fourth Plan:	1969-74	15,778.8	335.5	278.0	613.5
		(100)	(2.1)	(1.8)	(3.9)
Fifth Plan:	1974-9	39,426.2	760.8	491.8	1252.6
		(100)	(1.9)	(1.2)	(3.1)
Annual Plan:	1979-80	12,176.5	223.1	118.5	341.6
		(100)	(1.8)	(1.0)	(2.8)
Sixth Plan:	1980-5	1,09,291.7	2,025.2	1,387.0	3,412.2
		(100)	(1.8)	(1.3)	(3.1)
Seventh Plan:	1985-90	2,18,729.6	3,688.6	3,120	6,809.4
		(100)	(1.7)	(1.4)	(3.1)

Notes: 1. Figures in parentheses indicate percentages to total.
2. Health includes Minimum Needs Programme/Rural Programme, Control of Communicable Diseases, Hospitals and Dispensaries, Medical Education and Training, Indian Council of Medical Research, Indian System of Medicine and Homeopathic Medicines, Employees Insurance and other programmes.
Source: *Economic Survey 1991-2* and Planning Commission.

In the 1980s, quite a few interesting shifts took place in the area of health strategies. Considering the difficulties of cost and personnel in attaining the goals of 'Health for All by AD 2000', a shift from 'primary health care' to 'selective' primary health care was accepted. This gave small attention to maternal health (Banerji 1984). The 'child survival' strategies introduced by UNICEF, also, had little to contribute to the health of the mothers.

When 'maternal health' was receiving less and less attention in planning, the Working Group on Population Policy of 1980 had already proposed something different. It considered, 'Women as the best votaries of family welfare programme' and replaced the view of 'motherhood' with 'womanhood'. Through the Seventh Plan period, this has been extended to 'women's upliftment' and documented in the Eighth Plan. It

TABLE 2. PLAN ALLOCATIONS FOR HEALTH SECTOR (RS IN CRORES)

Allocations	1951-6 I	1956-61 II	1961-6 III	1966-9 Annual	1969-74 IV	1974-9 V	1980-5 VI	1986-91 VII
Health	90.3 (64.5)	146.0 (64.9)	150.0 (60.2)	93.9 (41.6)	433.5 (37.1)	796.5 (34.1)	1821.1 (27.0)	3392.2 (25.8)
Hospitals, Dispensaries and PHC	(17.9)	(16.0)	(14.9)	(11.1)	(7.6)	(6.7)	(10.7)	(10.5)
Control of communicable Diseases	(16.5)	(28.4)	(27.7)	(10.2)	(11.0)	(11.5)	(7.8)	(7.7)
Education and Training	(15.4)	(16.0)	(14.1)	(9.6)	(8.5)	(4.8)		(1.3)
Others	(14.7)	(4.5)	(3.3)	(10.2)	(10.0)	(11.1)	(8.5)	(6.3)
Family Welfare	(0.5)	(1.3)	(10.8)	(36.7)	(27.3)	(22.1)	(15.0)	(24.7)
Water Supply and Sanitation	(35.0)	(33.8)	(28.9)	(21.7)	(35.2)	(43.8)	(58.0)	(50.5)
Grand Total	140.0	225.0	249.0	225.8	1,155.5	2,334.2	6,753.0	13,171.65

Note: Figures in parentheses are percentages to grand total.
Sources: Meera Chatterjee, *Implementing Health Policy*, Delhi, 1988; Health Statistics of India, 1988.

may be noted that the United Nations had officially recognized 'gender as a basic social category' in the Declaration of the International Decade for Women which ended in 1985.

EVOLUTION OF MATERNAL HEALTH SERVICES

Maternal health was highlighted in the recommendations of the Bhore Committee where the importance of the 'primary health unit' was recognized and discussed. The scheme was put into operation in 1952, with the principle of providing 'integrated' preventive, promotive and curative health care. Over time, the primary health centre has become the nucleus of the rural health services (Banerji 1985).

In the First Plan, health was considered fundamental to national progress. MCH was in the forefront then along with the Malaria Control Programme. Family planning had a much lower priority. Maternal and Child Welfare was shifted from missionary and charitable institutions and was integrated with the basic health services (GOI 1951).

The high priority of MCH continued through the Second Plan period, which aimed at reaching out to people. Special attention was given to improving the institutional facilities, specially the proposed primary health units and training of manpower. In the Second Plan, 2,100 maternal and child welfare centres became an integral part of the general health services in the rural areas, with missionary and charitable institutions continuing to supplement the extension projects of these centres. At the end of the Plan, each of such centres was serving a population of 10,000 to 25,000. Simultaneously, integration of the staff of the national programmes of communicable diseases at the 'maintenance' phase was proposed (GOI 1956).

The Third Plan period was marked by a very high priority to the family planning programme, and control of communicable diseases (including Tuberculosis Control Programme of 1962) received greater attention from the planners (GOI 1961). The aim was expansion of services to bring about improvement in people's health. The emphasis was on preventive and curative aspects, and referral services for MCH were extended at the primary health units. Orientation of the hospital staff engaged in MCH work was also improved during this period, but the Bhore Committee's recommendation to have one woman doctor, four public health nurses, four midwives and four trained *dais* at a primary health unit covering 20,000 population was not achieved. Even in the 1960s, each PHC had only one medical officer, a sanitary inspector, one health visitor, a compounder and four auxiliary nurse midwives (ANM) (Dutt 1965).

During this period, two separate evaluations of the primary health care scheme and health and family planning services were conducted.

The Health Survey and Planning Committee (also known as Mudaliar Committee), in its evaluation of the primary health care scheme, stressed that attention should be focused on strengthening the staffing of existing PHCs rather than increasing the number of PHCs (GOI 1962). The committee proposed that the population should be serviced by mobile services. The strengthened PHCs would render preventive and curative services and take over the maintenance phase of the programmes for controlling communicable diseases. In practice, however, the number of PHCs increased in association with the adoption of extension approach in the family planning programme.

At the time, ANMs were responsible for both MCH and family planning work among rural women while family planning health assistants were doing family planning advocacy among men. They were supervised by a lady health visitor and a block extension educator. Similarly, there were workers and supervisors for malaria surveillance too. Meanwhile the Chaddha Committee report of 1963 (GOI 1963) proposed that the health and family planning services be integrated and served through male and female multipurpose workers, each serving a population of 10,000 at the initial stage. The committees's recommendations, however, were counter-productive, since the goal of health service clashed with that of family planning service. In 1966, the UN Advisory Mission proposed delinking family planning from MCH. Accordingly, ANMs who were working at village level for MCH, nutrition and family planning were relieved of the responsibilities of MCH and nutrition (UN 1966). Targets were set for the family planning programme, reinforced with threats and penalties affecting the employment and security of the ANM. In 1968, however, reversion was proposed once again (Banerji 1971).

Thus, the Third Plan witnessed an attempt at integration of the services for family planning, control of communicable diseases and MCH at the PHC level. The result was that on account of the target-oriented pressure of family planning work, MCH work was ignored.

During the years 1966-9, five-year planning was abandoned in favour of Annual Plans. These Annual Plans paid special attention to the growth of the family planning programme which continued over the Fourth Plan period (GOI 1966, 1967, 1968).

At the end of the Fourth Plan, targets for MCH were also set as recommended by the MCH Advisory Committee. In maternal health services, targets were set for immunization of pregnant mothers against tetanus, and also for the prophylaxis programme against nutritional anaemia (GOI 1990). Provision of preventive and curative health services in rural areas through establishment of PHC in each block, augmentation of the training of medical and para-medical personnel and control of communicable diseases occupied the attention of the planners.

In 1973, the Committee on Multipurpose Workers (Kartar Singh Committee) had reviewed the functioning of the PHCs and criticized the separation of the duties of various health workers and the poor coordination among them. The committee suggested that the smallest unit of population could be better served by coordinating these programmes and pooling the personnel. A scheme for Multipurpose Workers was proposed in which maternal health work became one of the many activities of the primary worker (GOI 1973).

The Fifth Plan paid considerable attention to MCH, and also sought to remove the rural-urban disparity in health care services. A Minimum Needs Programme was launched with the aim of meeting the needs of the poorest. The package provided elements of health, family planning, nutrition, environmental improvement and water supply apart from elementary adult education, roads, electrification in rural areas and housing for the landless labourers (GOI 1979). During this Plan period, the number of doctors serving PHC increased considerably, as also the number of PHCs and subcentres. In keeping with the people-oriented strategies of 'Health for All by AD 2000' the community health volunteers (CHV) joined the PHC network to make services more meaningful for the community and the *dai* training programme was initiated and was supposed to help the MCH work (GOI 1991).

The Sixth Plan had proposed health to be viewed in totality as a part of the strategy of human development. Horizontal and vertical linkages were to be established among all the integrated programmes such as water supply, environmental sanitation, hygiene, nutrition, education, family planning and maternal and child welfare (GOI 1979).

To attain this, the Plan emphasized infrastructural development and integration of services at the PHC level. To bring down the high morbidity and mortality rates among infants and mothers, the Plan emphasized improved health and nutritional status through various extension programmes for immunization, prophylaxis or supplementary nutrition. Nevertheless, the performance of the MCH programme during this Plan period, particularly in the field of immunization and antenatal care, was 'far from satisfactory' (GOI 1985). Measures for strengthening the programme and increasing the child survival rates were considered essential for the success of the MCH programme.

The Seventh Plan perspective was based on similar considerations. Thus, within MCH, child survival, intersectoral coordination and strengthening of infrastructure were emphasized to attain the goals of 'Health for All by AD 2000'. Special emphasis was given to 'women's health care' in the hope that raising health consciousness along with economic activities would enable women to actively participate in the entire process of socio-economic development, including health. During this period, AIDS (Acquired Immuno Deficiency Syndrome) emerged as a new public health problem in the country and the national programme to contain this new menace was launched in 1986.

IMPLICATIONS OF PLANNING FOR WOMEN'S HEALTH

Given the high priority to MCH in health planning during the 1950s, followed by its integration with the general health services, good potential for catering to maternal health was created. But the task of providing health services to mothers and children became complicated when MCH got intermingled with other programmes at the PHC level. In the name of integration, the constant shuttling between unipurpose and multipurpose workers at the primary level has led to confusion and seriously undermined efficiency.

In the 1940s, the Sokhey Committee had expressed concern for women's health by considering their economic role too. The five-year health plans, however, did not reflect such concern till the mid-1980s. In the Seventh and Eighth Plan documents 'women's health' has been given a separate identity, 'to enable them to participate in the process of socio-economic development including health'. The reality is something else. Although MMR has dropped from 12.4 per 1,000 live births in 1936 to 1.9 at the end of the 1980s, causes of maternal mortality such as anaemia and puerperal sepsis have got little attention (Soman 1994). During 1985-90, for example, puerperal sepsis contributed to 10.37 per cent of the total maternal deaths as against 31.95 per cent in 1936; the figure for anaemia remains at 19.10 per cent as against 23.3 per cent in 1936. There may be differences in the quality of data collected after a gap of nearly five decades, but such bias, if any, would be equally present for both causes of maternal mortality discussed here. In other words, though aseptic conditions of delivery have improved, anaemia continues to be an important factor for maternal deaths. The decline in the proportion of puerperal sepsis may have been a result of an improvement in the people's living conditions. A rise in the level of consciousness may also have increased their access to health care services. The relatively unchanged ratio of home delivery to 'institutional delivery' presumably indicates a better functioning of the trained *dais* who are closer to the communities. Moreover, this phenomenon may also be due to the possible decline in the virulence of the causative agents in the environment. Nevertheless, the figures reveal that women's general ill-health leading to maternal death remained nearly stagnant over the decades of health interventions. The declining sex ratio also reflects on the poor social and health status women have (GOI 1992).

A time-trend analysis of the causes of maternal mortality since the 1970s reveals that within the largely unchanged pattern of maternal deaths in rural India, avoidable causes like anaemia continue to account for a large proportion of such deaths (Soman 1994). In an evaluation of the Anaemia Prophylaxis programme in the country, the Indian Council of Medical Research noted: 'the existing nutritional anaemia prophylaxis programme has not made any noticeable impact on reducing the incidence of anaemia, despite being in operation for fifteen years'. To ameliorate the situation the Council emphasized the use of functionaries at PHC level. Ironically, the ICMR expected the ANMs to answer the queries of mothers in addition to other functions, such as monitoring and reporting in close interaction with the trained birth attendants, village health guides, *anganwadi* workers of Integrated Child Development Services and also with the local NGOs. This was in regard to the Anaemia Prophylaxis programme *per se*, when the ANM's duties outside the programme are multifarious. This is an instance of the mismatch between recommendations and reality that continues in health planning.

The latest Plan document also admits the continuing inadequacies of the rural infrastructure. It states: 'As much as approximately two-thirds of the total expenditure on health services is spent on personnel. Yet health manpower planning, production and management which constitute key elements for effective implementation of health programmes have not received enough attention' (GOI 1990).

The document accepts that there is a mismatch between the requirement and availability of health personnel of different categories.

The sum and substance of the convolutions in planning inevitably leads to the conclusion that there is a need for understanding women's health in its totality, embracing 'maternal health' as well as the general 'ill-health' of women together. Since the mid-1980s, 'maternal health' has been supplemented by 'women's health care' in health planning. The current discussion on bringing reproductive health services (covering more problems such as reproductive tract infection, problems of sterility and abortion) to the community through the primary health care network (World Bank 1995), therefore, also needs careful reflection. Given the importance of infrastructural facilities as a prerequisite to any attempt at rendering reproductive health services to women, there is an urgent need to improve the existing health infrastructure, especially in rural areas.

NGO INTERVENTION

NGO intervention in health has been a dynamic process, ranging from charity orientation to self-reliance and people's involvement in their own development; from hospital-based medical care to health care at the doorsteps.

The NGOs' relationship with the government health programmes had been supportive at the beginning of the planning process. Later, however, it expressed discontent with the government's inability to fulfil the tasks of development. In the mid-1970s, the government encouraged the NGOs to take over some health programmes which included operation of a number of PHCs, evolution of methods of delivery of health care through village health workers and their training. In health planning during the 1980s, the strength of NGOs was realized and relied upon by the planners. Active participation of rural agencies was encouraged in areas including primary health care and MCH services (Bhatia 1993).

The NGOs, despite facing criticism and having their own limitations, specially of 'inadequate coverage' and 'lack of uniformity', continue to draw their strength from people's involvement in preventive and curative health care delivery. They have gathered experience, reconfirming the proposal of decentralized and people-based health system by the joint committee of ICSSR/ICMR. They have also learnt that health care cannot operate in isolation; there is also need for decentralization of all sectors of development, which is the essence of Panchayati Raj (Antia and Bhatia 1993).

In conclusion, one may draw attention to the major trends in the philosophy of current health interventions. On one hand, there are international forces influencing State health policies, and on the other, there are various attempts to bring 'the people' to the centre-stage. Amidst these pulls, how does one assess the performance in the area of health in the light of the Bhore Committee recommendations made more than half a century ago? Does one reorient one's priorities? The answer will depend on the nature of access to good health that women of India will have in coming years.

REFERENCES

Antia, N.H. and K. Bhatia (eds.), 1993. *People's Health in People's Hands*. The Foundation for Research in Community Health, Bombay.

Banerji, D., 1971. *Family Planning in India: A Critique and A Perspective*, People's Publishing House, New Delhi.

——————, 1984. *Primary Health Care: Selective or Comprehensive*, World Health Forum, Vol. 5, pp. 312-15.

——————, 1985. *Health and Family Planning Services in India: An Epidemiological, Socio-cultural and Political Analysis and a Perspective*, Lok Paksh, New Delhi.

Basu, D.D., 1970. *Shorter Constitution of India*, Calcutta.

Bhatia, Kavita, 1993. 'The NGO movement in Health', in N.H. Antia and K. Bhatia, 1993.

Dutt, P.R., 1965. *Rural Health Services in India: Primary Health Centres*, Central Health Education Bureau, New Delhi.

Government of India, 1946. *Health Survey and Development Committee: Report*, Vols. I-IV, Manager of Publications, New Delhi.

——————, 1951. *First Five-year Plan*, Planning Commission, New Delhi.

——————, 1956. *Second Five-year Plan*, Planning Commission, New Delhi.

——————, 1961. *Third Five-year Plan*, Planning Commission, New Delhi.

——————, 1962. *Report of the Health Survey and Planning Committee* (Mudaliar Committee), Ministry of Health, New Delhi.

——————, 1963. *Report of the Committee of Integration of Health Services*, Ministry of Health, New Delhi.

——————, 1966, 1967, 1968. *Annual Plans*, Planning Commission, New Delhi.

——————, 1968. *Report on the Basic Health Services*, Ministry of Health and Family Planning, New Delhi.

——————, 1970. *Fourth Five-year Plan*, Planning Commission, New Delhi.

——————, 1972-3. *Annual Report of Swasthya Aur Parivar Niyojan Mantralaya*, New Delhi, pp. 76-8.

——————, 1973. *Report of the Committee on Multi-purpose Workers Under Health and Family Planning Programme* (Kartar Singh Committee), Ministry of Health and Family Planning, New Delhi.

——————, 1976. *National Population Policy*, Ministry of Health and Family Welfare, New Delhi.

——————, 1979. *Draft Sixth Five-year Plan (Revised)*, Planning Commission, New Delhi.

———, 1980a. *Report of the Working Group on Population Policy*, Planning Commission, New Delhi.
———, 1980b. *Sixth Five-year Plan*, Planning Commission, New Delhi.
———, 1985. *Seventh Five-year Plan*, Vol. II, Planning Commission, New Delhi.
———, 1989. *Report of the Working Group on Anaemia*, Ministry of Health and Family Welfare, New Delhi, pp. 1-10.
———, 1990. *Eighth Five Year Plan*, Planning Commission, New Delhi, pp. 322, 329.
———, 1991. *Health Information of India*, Central Bureau of Health Information, Directorate General of Health Services, Ministry of Health and Family Welfare, New Delhi.
———, 1992. *Trends in Sex Ratio in India: 1901 to 1991*, Health Information of India, Central Bureau of Health Intelligence, Directorate General of Health Services, Ministry of Health and Family Welfare, New Delhi.
Indian Council of Social Science Research and Indian Council of Medical Research, 1981. *Health for All: An Alternative Strategy*, Indian Institute of Education, Pune.
National Planning Committee, 1948. *Report of the Sub-Committee on National Health* (Sokhey Committee), Vora Publishers, Bombay.
Qadeer, Imrana, 1995. 'Population and Structural Readjustment: Games Nations Play', *Voice* (Bangalore) I(2), pp. 18-22.
Rao, Mohan, 1990. *The Indian Family Planning Programme: A Retrospective*, Paper presented at the Indian Peoples Science Congress, Bangalore.
Soman, Krishna, 1994. 'Trends in Maternal Mortality', *Economic and Political Weekly* 29(44).
United Nations, 1966. *Report of the Advisory Mission on the Family Planning Programme in India*, New York.
World Bank, 1995. India's Family Welfare Programme: Toward a Reproductive and Child Health Approach, Population and Human Resources Operations Division, South Asia Country Department (Bhutan, India, Nepal), pp. 12-17.

Health Sector Financing in the Context of Women's Health

RAVI DUGGAL

PROLOGUE

In the last decade or so, women's health has been receiving special attention the world over. From the Nairobi UN Conference, through the Cairo ICPD and to the recently concluded Beijing Conference, women's health and health care has been an important agenda item which has taken a growing share of attention, and especially so reproductive health. And the catch lies here.

While recognizing the importance of reproductive health, especially in a country like India which still has relatively high fertility, an overwhelming proportion of deliveries being conducted at homes, often in unhygienic conditions, a supposed unconcern for gynaecological morbidities and an embarrassingly high proportion of abortions being done illegally, it is even more important to emphasize the need for making available comprehensive health services to women as a group for their special needs. However, the danger of beginning with reproductive health is narrowing down the focus to the uterus, precisely what the women's health movements want to avoid. And pushing for making reproductive health a special programme under the State's primary health care programme is likely to end up the same way as earlier versions of women's health programmes like the MCH programme or safe motherhood have, i.e. in targets for population control programmes, especially hazardous contraceptives like injectables and implants.

Thus, the demand must begin with provision of easily accessible and comprehensive health care for all, with a clear recognition and provision for women's special needs, as well as of other vulnerable groups like children, senior citizens, tribals, etc. Natural and social justice demands that society must provide for a basic decent human life. This becomes even more urgent in countries where poverty is rampant, where social provisions like health, education, housing, public transportation and other public utilities are not available to a large majority of the population.

HEALTH SECTOR IN INDIA

Before we look into gender inequalities in the context of health care, it is important to review the overall availability of health care services in the country.

Going by statistics, India perhaps has adequate health care infrastructure available. We have about 8 lakh hospital beds and 10 lakh qualified medical practitioners, that is 85 beds per lakh population and 110 doctors per lakh population. If distributed rationally, this is a fairly adequate number. But then reality is different.

First, 80 per cent of the qualified practitioners are in the private sector and they operate without any regulations or control whatsoever, and, of course, for profit. The private health sector market is completely supply induced and the patient is totally at the mercy of the practitioner's whims and fancies. *Secondly*, 60 per cent of those in private practice are trained in systems other than modern medicine or allopathy and yet a very large majority of these other system practitioners (Ayurveda, Homeopathy, Unani, Siddha, etc.) treat patients with modern medicines (of course, some allopaths also indulge in cross practice). *Thirdly*, two-thirds of private practitioners are located in urban areas when 70 per cent of the population resides in rural areas. *Fourthly*, the public health sector, too, has an urban bias. As much as 80 per cent of public sector medical care services and consequently as much of the budget for medical care is for urban areas. The rural areas have primary health centres (PHCs) which provide mostly preventive and promotive services like immunization, ante-natal services and family planning services, but medical care which is the people's main demand and need is not available in rural areas, as even four-fifths of the public hospitals and beds are located in urban areas.

Apart from the formal health sector discussed above, there is the informal sector of hereditary, caste-based and/or unqualified/untrained practitioners of various kinds. Their number, though not known, is as large or perhaps larger than the formal sector—various types of unqualified practitioners ranging from downright quacks to paramedics, *dais*, *bhagats*, voodoos, witch doctors, herbalists, a variety of others and of course the local disease/technique specialists like abortionists, white-discharge experts, jaundice specialists, snakebite specialists, etc.

WOMEN AND THE HEALTH SECTOR

Given the above dismal picture of health care in India, not much can be expected in favour of women as clients of the health care system. The core attention of both the private and public health system towards women is to view them as mothers. While the private nursing home sector mostly comprises maternity homes, the public health sector's major concern *vis-à-vis* women is to prevent them from becoming mothers. While the private maternity homes cater to the urban population and the middle classes (about 500 lakh women in the reproductive ages) the public sector's health services offer family planning services (overwhelmingly tubectomy and IUCD) in both rural and urban areas covering over 10 crore couples. The maternity services available under the public sector, especially in rural areas, are mostly through paramedics like auxiliary nurse midwives (ANMs) or trained *dais*.

Beyond the above and some other occasional services like antenatal care and abortion services (both within the context of family planning), little else is available to women to address their general and other gender-specific health care needs. Of course, the informal sector practitioners do cater to some specific needs of women like abortion, white discharge, psychic problems (what patriarchal literature calls hysteria), etc., but very little of it is documented to enable a discussion or make comments. Some efforts are definitely being made to understand the contribution and/or harm of such providers. Some NGOs and women's groups have put in efforts to document this and have even helped in improving the skills of such practitioners.

This gross neglect begins with defining women's health care needs and their low status in society. Women in India, and especially those in rural areas, given their general living conditions and the double burden on their shoulders, have never publicly voiced their concern over their reproductive, sexual and gynaecological health needs. Even something as obvious as menstruation is grossly neglected and this has serious consequences because many diseases in our country are related to blood loss—tuberculosis, malaria, dysentery, *kala azar*, hookworm—and hence makes anaemia an extremely important concern of women's health which currently receives little attention.

The health system, as indicated earlier, views women's health only in terms of their uterus. Thus, historically all health programmes designed specifically for women have been related to MCH, family planning (contraception), child survival, safe motherhood, etc. Tragically, even this narrow focused approach has failed to provide women services related to safe pregnancy, maternity, contraception, etc. High maternal mortality and high levels of unsafe, unhygienic births, especially in the rural areas, are commonplace.

The poor overall coverage of both private and public health sectors taken together for the various MCH services as found during the 42nd Round of the National Sample Survey in 1986-7 and the NFHS in 1992-3 may be seen in Table 1. The rural-urban and the strong class differences are also worth noting. While the NFHS data are not strictly comparable with the NSS data, the improvement in coverage, especially of immunization and ante-natal care, over the period due to perhaps the mission approach and higher allocation of resources, is also worth noting.

The health workers and infrastructure available even for these limited programmes is grossly inadequate and of poor quality. In rural areas, the PHCs and subcentres are so poorly equipped for even these meagre services that doctors and nurses are unwilling to risk even a normal delivery. Ironically, even tubectomy, the government's most favoured 'health' programme, is not available on demand to women at the PHC because it is done only in a camp where extra facilities/resources are made available. Further, the obsession of public health services with family planning has discredited the entire public health system in the rural areas.

Even in urban areas where infrastructure and physical access to public health services is relatively far better, women get a raw deal. Let alone their special health needs, even women's general health needs do not get the necessary attention. This becomes evident when we see the unfavourable ratio of beds assigned to women as well as the actual utilization by women of both outdoor and indoor services. Further, many studies have also indicated that women carry a high burden of chronic ailments in the absence of care or total neglect of illnesses. This situation is mainly due to women's health needs getting the least priority in the family.

Given the existing patterns of health care provision, access to general health care needs for the masses is extremely limited. More so, current trends of increased privatization and the concept of selective primary care for public services is going to worsen the situation for the impoverished majority. And within this, a place for women's health care needs gets further diluted or even more focused towards fertility control.

TABLE 1. MCH SERVICES UTILIZATION (PUBLIC AND PRIVATE SECTORS) ACROSS CLASSES AND RURAL-URBAN AREAS: ALL INDIA PERCENTAGE COVERAGE 1987 AND 1993

Class	RURAL								URBAN						
	Completed Immunization		Maternity Care		Births		Completed Immunization		Maternity Care		Births				
	Polio	Triple	ANC	PNC	Domi-ciliary	Hospital	Polio	Triple	ANC	PNC	Domi-ciliary	Hospital			
1987—NSS															
Bottom 10%	7.24	4.41	17.36	10.35	86.75	8.91	14.31	9.54	39.04	21.16	62.05	33.75			
Top 10%	25.76	20.44	41.667	20.36	55.24	39.03	59.26	51.16	94.05	58.32	8.75	84.25			
All	10.77	7.56	21.15	12.60	80.52	13.53	26.82	20.51	46.83	23.76	46.85	48.20			
Difference Between															
Top and Bottom (Times)	3.5	4.6	2.4	2.0	0.6	4.4	4.1	5.4	2.4	2.7	0.1	2.5			
1993—NHFS	48.4	46.6	56.7	-	83.0	16.0	70.2	68.8	81.1	-	41.5	57.6			

Source: 1987—NSS: Compiled from *Sarvekshana*, 47 (April-June 1991), Tables 2R, 2U, 5R, 6R, 6U, 7R, 7U, 8R, 8U. Data are from the NSS 42nd Round Survey—1987, and NFHS 1993. Compiled from National Family Health Survey—India 1992-3, Tables 9.1, 9.5, 9.11, IIPS, Bombay, 1995.

HEALTH CARE SPENDING

While the problem starts at the family level itself wherein women's health needs are least important, the actual neglect is due to inadequate allocations by the State for health care services. The world over it has been proved that with universal access and assurance of basic health care, women's access to health care services has become equitable, at least for general health services, if not for their special health needs as women.

With the present level of allocation by the State to the health sector of less than 1 per cent of the GDP, not even one-fourth of the health needs of the people are met. The State's lack of commitment to provide health care for its citizens is reflected not only in the inadequacy of the health infrastructure and low levels of financing, but also a declining people's support to the demand for health care. This situation has become more prominent since the early 1980s, coinciding with the process of liberalization and opening up of the Indian economy to world markets. Evidence of this is presented in Table 2.

Medical care (hospitals and dispensaries) and control of communicable diseases are crucial areas of concern both in terms of what people demand as priority areas of health care as well as what existing socioeconomic conditions demand. As with overall public health spending, both these programmes also show declining trends in fiscal allocations in the 1980s and 1990s. In fact, in the case of disease programmes, this decline is surprising because of the large foreign assistance for AIDS and blindness control. This then means that for other crucial diseases like tuberculosis, the State's increasing disinterest in allocating resources for the health sector (family planning being an exception) is also reflected in investment expenditure—there has been a very large decline in capital expenditure during the 1990s. Further, if we take into account the growth rate of inflation we would get a large negative growth for the most recent years.

Looking at these same ratios across states, we see that not one state government shows a significant trend different from the overall trends (Duggal et al. 1995). This only goes to show how strongly the Central government influences the states' financing decisions even in a sector where the constitutional responsibility is vested with the state governments and the centre's grants are only about 10 per cent of state government spending. This 'united action' has been possible because health care policy-making and planning is largely done at the level of the central government and hence the latter can use arm-twisting tactics. This

TABLE 2. SELECTED PUBLIC HEALTH EXPENDITURE 1980-95 (%)

Year	1980-1	1985-6	1991-2	1992-3	1993-4	1994-5
Health expenditure as per cent of total government expenditure	3.29	3.29	3.11	2.71	2.71	2.63
Expenditure on medical care as per cent of total health expenditure	43.30	37.82	26.78	27.66	27.46	25.75
Expenditure on disease programmes as per cent of total health expenditure	12.96	11.69	10.59	10.84	10.41	9.51
Expenditure on family planning as per cent of total health expenditure	11.94	17.94	19.39	16.54	16.88	17.27
Capital expenditure as per cent of total health expenditure	8.15	9.23	8.43	4.20	4.67	4.46
Absolute annual per capita growth rate of health expenditure in per cent	15	21	11	13	17	7

Source: Duggal, Nandraj and Vadair (1995).

structure of planning reduces any initiative that a state government may want to take for reallocating resources to favour people's demands for health care. The result is that people do not get satisfactory services from the public system and hence get discouraged to use it.

Low levels of public spending for health and low utilization of public health services are closely linked. The 1987 NSSO survey on utilization of health care facilities reveals that for outpatient care, public services were utilized for only 26 per cent of the cases. But it also reveals that states with a higher per capita public health expenditure had better rates of public facility use. Further, states having a weak penetration of the private health sector had very high public health facility utilization (NSSO 1987). Similar trends have also been found in studies done by NCAER, NIHFW, FRCH and others (Berman and Khan 1992; World Bank 1994). Still, as yet the use of public hospitals is higher because 70 per cent of hospital beds are in the public domain. But with 80 per cent hospitals being in urban areas the rural residents, who constitute three-fourths of the population, have tremendous difficulties in obtaining such care.

During the 1980s, the State did put in genuine efforts at expansion of the rural health infrastructure (even though for strengthening the outreach of family planning), but it is precisely during this period, as we have seen above, that there was a declining trend in public spending on health care. This same period also witnessed a massive growth rate of expansion of the private health sector (Jesani and Ananthram 1993). The database of the NIPFP shows that real growth rates of public health spending have declined rapidly during the 1980s, and more so for central government spending (Table 3).

Since the 1980s, India's debt burden and interest payments have galloped at a rapid rate. In this state of the economy the social sector is the first to be axed. Under structural adjustment since 1991, there has been further compression in government spending in an effort to bring down the fiscal deficit to the desired level. The budget expenditures of the central government have declined from 19.8 per cent of the GDP in 1990-1 to 16.58 per cent in 1993-4. This compression again has been more severe for the central health sector. The NIPFP database gives evidence of the compression that has taken place over the last decade. It shows that the state's share in health expenditure has increased and that of the centre declined drastically. Further, the breakdown of central assistance to states reveals that central programmes or centrally funded programmes are of a preventive and promotive nature. Decline of spending on these programmes means serious consequences for the nation's health, especially considering that the private sector has no interest in preventive and promotive care (Tables 4 and 5).

Another serious problem in public health spending is the large and increasing proportion of the expenditure on salaries. This explains in part the poor use of public health services because non-salary components like medicines, fuel, equipment, etc. are inadequately funded. The NIPFP database shows that commodity purchases declined steadily from 29 per cent of total expenditure in 1978 to 22 per cent in 1988 as did capital expenditure from 9 per cent to 7 per cent. It also reveals that real growth rate in salary expenditure during that period was 9.8 per cent and that of commodities was 5.3 per cent (Tulasidhar 1992). NCAER also found in a district and municipal level study in four states that non-salary inputs ranged between 5 per cent and 21 per cent (World Bank 1994). This declining share of non-salary spending will aggravate

TABLE 3. REAL GROWTH RATE IN HEALTH CARE EXPENDITURE (%)

Centre/Stae Govts	1974-82	1982-9
15 Major States	9.99	8.42
Central Government	12.13	3.44
Centre + States	10.03	8.22

Source: Tulasidhar, 1992.

TABLE 4. SHARE OF CENTRE AND STATES IN HEALTH EXPENDITURE (%)

Centre/State Govts	1974-82	1982-9	1992-3
States' Own Funds	71.6	79.9	85.7
Grants from Centre	19.9	5.8	3.3
Centre's Expenditure	8.5	14.3	11.0

Source: V.B. Tulasidhar, *Structural Adjustment Programme: Its impact on the Health Sector*, NIPFP, 1992 (mimeo).

TABLE 5. SHARE OF CENTRAL GRANTS IN STATE HEALTH SPENDING (%)

Year	Medical and Public Health	Public Health	Disease Programmes	Family Welfare
1984-5	6.73	27.92	41.47	99.00
1989-90	3.91	16.66	29.12*	74.51
1992-3	3.70	17.17	18.50	88.59

Note: *Figure for 1988-9.
Source: Same as in Table 4.

the inefficiencies within the system, further damaging the already poor reputation of public health services.

The analysis and evidence presented above clearly indicate the urgency of stemming the decline in public spending on health care and taking appropriate fiscal actions to improve the efficiency and effectiveness of the public health care system.

The major problem of health sector development in India, especially in the last two decades, has been that new programmes are begun and new facilities started with Plan funds (and an increasing amount with foreign borrowings) but their future sustenance is not completely assured by additional non-Plan allocations. Health being a state subject, its sustainability is dependent on allocations made by the state. The centre has major control of Plan resources and the states want to grab as large a share as they can. Therefore, in the initial years of the Plan scheme they are willing to provide matching grants, but when it is time to take charge of the programmes they shirk their responsibilities. The programme then continues to remain a part of the Plan resources with the result that new investments get affected because these old Plan commitments do not get transferred to non-Plan budgets. Further, states have a tendency to divert programme funds away from components they are earmarked for. This is largely due to the restricted role they play in policy-making and planning.

This mismatch of centre-state priorities has proved very expensive as funds are wasted on inadequately provided tasks causing allocative inefficiencies and failure of the programme to fulfil its objectives completely. For example, a recent GOI-WHO-SIDA evaluation of the tuberculosis programme revealed the following:

— inadequate coverage of TB services in peripheral health institutions;
— underfunding of drugs to the extent that the effective supply was for only one-third of the cases detected;
— over-reliance on X-ray diagnosis with the result that cases tended to concentrate in district TB centre;
— ineffective laboratory services due to insufficient human hours of the microscopist at the PHC; and
— inefficient drug distribution mechanism which results in a very high drop-out rate after initial symptomatic relief to the patient.

As regards spending specifically for women's health care, there is only the MCH programme which gets merely 2 per cent of the national health budget. This apart, there is the family planning programme which is targeted almost solely at women (tubectomy and IUCD) but it does not contribute much to women's health care needs; if at all, it has caused more harm than good. As we have seen earlier, family planning budgets have grown at a steady pace but the corresponding decline in fertility rates has not been commensurate with such high investments for this high-profile programme of the State. In 1993-4, for instance, Rs 1,072.5 crore (excluding MCH) were spent on family planning, which was 14.93 per cent of the national health budget. In the remaining expenditure, which is the core health budget, women's stake is extremely limited because of the problems discussed in an earlier section.

WHAT CAN BE DONE?

The above picture looks rather dismal. It must be recognized that it is a consequence of the overall underdevelopment. The new economic policy and structural adjustment have not been helpful, and especially so for the social sectors. What does this mean for the health sector and the people of this country?

Health care access and availability in India has a peculiar public-private mix which generates a political economy that makes the health sector purchasing-power dependent. This is a contradiction given that the large majority do not have purchasing capacities even to sustain adequate nutritional requirements. In a country where nearly half the population struggles under severe poverty conditions and another one-half of the remaining manages at the subsistence level, it is a sad state of affairs that social needs like health and education have to be more often than not bought in the marketplace. Thus, when we discuss issues in health financing, we must not restrict ourselves to money matters but highlight macro issues like poverty, poor availability of public services and strong penetration of private sector in the provision of health care.

Therefore, when we look at issues in health care and its financing, we must begin with this reality of general impoverishment on the one hand and the market-led for-profit private health sector on the other. While the public health sector, accounting for less than one-fifth of the overall health expenditure, is financed almost wholly through tax revenues, the dominant private health sector is financed by people directly through fee-for-services. Insurance- and employer-supported financing, as yet, accounts for a very small proportion of the total funding of the health sector.

ISSUES OF CONCERN

Defining primary care. Primary health care needs to be defined in terms of people's needs and a minimum decent level of provision. Primary care services should include at least the following:

— general practitioner/family physician services for personal health care;
— first level referral hospital care and basic specialist services, including dental and ophthalmic services;

- immunization services against vaccine-preventable diseases;
- maternity services for safe pregnancy, delivery and post-natal care;
- pharmaceutical services—supply of only rational and essential drugs as per accepted standards;
- epidemiological services, including laboratory services, surveillance and control of major diseases with the aid of continuous surveys, information management and public health measures;
- ambulance services;
- contraceptive services; and
- health education.

It must be emphasized that the above minimum care must be seen as a comprehensive programme and not compartmentalized into separate programmes as is done currently. These comprehensive primary care services must be common to the rural and urban areas and should be sensitive to special needs of groups like women, the elderly, children, tribals, etc.

The urgent need to strengthen, restructure and reorient public health services. The urban bias in medical care provision by the State needs to be removed. The PHCs and subcentres (SCs) need to be thoroughly reoriented to meet people's needs of medical care and not be obsessed with family planning alone. Facilities for medical care need to be substantially enhanced at the PHCs both in terms of personnel and supplies. While supplies can be increased through larger budgetary allocations, the difficulty would be in getting personnel to work in the public system. Since private individual practice is the norm, it becomes necessary to involve such practitioners to join a public-sponsored health care programme on a predefined payment system like a fixed capitation fee per family registered with the practitioner. Such a system needs to be evolved both in the rural and urban areas. This would mean a fivefold increase in primary care costs which may be partly financed from within the existing resources and the remaining from the organized sectors of the economy, including insurance, and special health-related taxes. Of course, this would mean a lot of restructuring, including stronger regulations, control and a mechanism for regular audit of the system's functioning. This is the only way of guaranteeing universal access to health care and achieving 'health for all'. The bottom line would be no direct payments by patients at the time of receiving care. All payments would be made through a statutory authority which would be the monopoly buyer. People having the capacity to pay should be charged indirectly through taxes, insurance premia, levies, etc. Such restructuring would not disturb the autonomy of the individual practitioner or the private hospitals except that it would strive to eliminate irrational and unnecessary practices, demand some amount of relocation of practitioners, standardize and rationalize costs and incomes, eliminate quackery and demand accountability from the providers.

Making the public health sector efficient, cost-effective and socially accountable. The response to the malaise of the public health services should not be 'privatization'. We already have a large, exploitative and unsustainable private health sector. What makes the private health sector 'popular' in usage is its better access—irrespective of quality, a personalized interface, availability at convenience, and non-bureaucratic nature. The public health services by contrast are bureaucratic, having poor access—especially in rural areas, have often inconvenient timings, are generally impersonal, often do not have requisite supplies like drugs, etc., and are plagued by nepotism and corruption. There is considerable scope for improvement of public health services with better planning, reallocation of existing resources as well as pumping in additional resources—especially for non-salary expenditure, reducing waste and improving efficiency by better management practices and separation of primary, secondary and tertiary care through setting up of referral systems, improving working conditions of employees, etc. One good example of enhancing the value, efficiency and effectiveness of the existing system using the available resources is to assure that all medical graduates who pass out of public medical schools (80 per cent of all graduates every year) serve in the public system for say at least five years without which they should be denied the licence to practise as well as admission for post-graduate studies. After all the State is spending Rs 8,00,000 per medical graduate! This measure, if enacted by law, will itself make available 14,000 doctors every year for the public health care system. There can be many such macro-decisions which can help in making the existing resources more effective and useful. Further, public health services must be made accountable to the local communities they serve and the latter must both carry out social audit as well as ensure that the system works properly for the benefit of patients. As regards the private health sector, as mentioned above, there is an urgent need to regulate it, standardize charges, and have policies for location and distribution.

Modes of financing and payment. While the public sector is funded through tax revenues, the private sector relies mostly on fee-for-services. There is a growing trend of thought favouring at least partial user-charges or fee-for-services for public health services. This trend must be countered since in the given socio-economic conditions, such a policy would hit the majority very hard. WHO has been firm about States spending 5 per cent of GDP on health care. In India, the State does not spend even 1 per cent. So, the first effort must be to get the State to commit a much larger share for the health sector from existing resources. Additional revenues specifically for health budgets may be collected on the lines of profession tax in some states; funds for employment programmes, levies and cesses for health could be collected by local bodies; employers in the organized sector must be made to contribute for health care services; those with capacity to pay like organized sector employees, the middle and rich peasantry (so far completely untaxed), and other self-employed, must do so through insurance and other prepayment programmes. In a vast and varied country like India, no single system would work. What we would need is a combination of social insurance for the poor (premia paid by the State), employment-related insurance for the organized sector employees, voluntary insurance for other categories who can afford to pay and, of course, tax and related revenues. Further, payments of any kind at the point of provision of care must not exist as they usually are unfavourable to patients. Payments must be made to providers by a monopoly buyer of health services who can also command certain standard practices and maintain a minimum quality of care—payments could be made in a variety of ways such as capitation or fixed charges for a standard regimen of services, fee-for-service as per standardized rates. The move towards monopoly purchase of health services through insurance or other means, and payment to providers through this single channel is a logical and growing global trend. To achieve universal access to health care and relative equity, this is perhaps the only alternative available at present. But this of necessity implies the setting up of an organized system for which the State has to play the lead role and involve the large private sector within this universal health care paradigm if it is to be successful.

Apart from the above macro measures which require radical changes, many improvements are also possible within the existing framework of the health system. Thus, apart from substantially enhancing resources for the public health sector, there is also an urgent need to reorient spending and remove the allocative inefficiencies. This is possible in many ways:

(i) If the states play a more significant role in health care planning and measure the cost-effectiveness of intra-sectoral allocations within the programme, they can assure long-term sustenance and make the programme meaningful.
(ii) By ensuring that the non-salary inputs are maintained at an adequate level, especially stocks of essential drugs, maintenance of facilities and equipment, fuel, etc., which is efficient enough to attract patients.
(iii) By rationalizing the use of hospitals through a referral system. This can be achieved if primary care facilities are well equipped and better funded to meet the demands of basic health care.
(iv) By improving the mix of health care staff in the various facilities and programmes. For instance, improving the nurse-doctor ratio in hospitals can bring down considerably the unit cost of hospital services.
(v) By improving drug management and assuring that only rational and essential generic drugs are purchased. International experience shows that this reduces drug costs by half, and
(vi) By ensuring that allocations are based on actual requirements or needs and that once committed, funds are not diverted for other expenditures.

With regard to women's special health care needs, while special attention is necessary, it must be embedded within the framework of comprehensive health care services and not designed as a special/selective programme, because history tells us that special programmes become ends in themselves and develop their own vested interests. This has been especially true of programmes that were designed for women which ended targeting their uteruses to stop them from reproducing.

In conclusion, we must reassert the importance of much larger resources being allocated for public health care. Every effort must be made to approximate the WHO suggested guideline for spending 5 per cent of the GDP on health care. But this will not be possible if the private health sector is left unregulated and has no links with the public system. The consequence of leaving the private health sector out of the ambit of State planning has been that with the rapid growth of the private sector, the wealthy and the more articulate segments of the population increasingly seek care in the private sector and any support, social and political, for a national health system which may be there will get buried in demands for privatization, further running down the public sector and hence the interests of the poor. The global trend is to evolve an effective public-private mix which functions under a single umbrella of a monopoly buyer of health services, which can either be a statutory body constituted by an Act of Parliament, or an insurance group, or the State, or some combination of these. This creation of a single system which assures universal coverage with equity should be the not-too-distant goal in the reorganization of the country's health care services. Such reorganization will bring about tremendous savings to the economy, both in terms of cutting down wasteful expenditure, especially in the private sector (over-prescriptions, unnecessary tests, procedures and specialist referrals, etc.), and in improving the productivity of the population by assuring equitable access to health care for all.

REFERENCES

Berman, Peter and M.E. Khan (eds.), 1992. *Paying For India's Health Care*, Sage, New Delhi.

Duggal, Ravi, S. Nandraj and A. Vadair, 1995. 'Health Expenditure across States—Special Statistics Part I and II', *Economic and Political Weekly* 30(15, 16).

Jesani, Amar and S. Ananthram, 1993. *Private Sector and Privatization in Health Care Services*, FRCH, Bombay.

NSSO, 1987. *Morbidity and Utilization of Medical Services,* Report No. 364, National Sample Survey Organization, Government of India, New Delhi.

Tulasidhar, V.B., 1992. *State Financing of Health Care in India*, NIPFP, New Delhi.

World Bank, 1994. *Policy and Finance Strategies for Strengthening Primary Health Care Services—India*, Report No. 13042-IN, World Bank.

Gender Equality and Political Participation: Implications for Good Health

A.K. Shiva Kumar

INTRODUCTION

The recognition that people are a nation's wealth has led to an increasing acceptance of development as an enhancement of people's capabilities.[1] This has been interpreted very effectively in recent times by UNDP's Human Development Reports (HDRs), published annually since 1990, as a process of enlarging people's choices. The HDRs have argued that at all levels of development, the three essential choices are for people to lead a long and healthy life, to acquire knowledge, and to have access to resources needed for a decent standard of living.[2] Underlying the concept of human development is the strong notion of equality of opportunity for all people in society regardless of race, class, caste, gender, ethnicity, religion, or any other consideration. Development becomes unjust and discriminatory when certain groups in society are excluded from enjoying the benefits of development.

UNDP's *Human Development Report 1995* draws attention to one of the most distressing forms of discrimination, namely the persistence of gender inequalities in society. The report notes that even though there has been an enhancement of women's capabilities in every country, women and men still live in an unequal world. Assuring women and men equal rights assumes critical significance particularly in India, given the systematic discrimination against women and the persistence of a strong anti-female bias throughout the country. There is perhaps no more shameful statistic than that some 40 to 50 million girls and women are 'missing' from the Indian population.[3]

Often, discussions on ensuring equal opportunities for women and men tend to focus on social and economic rights. The primacy of social and economic rights assumes an automatic justification, particularly in poor societies, given the profile of human deprivations that is frequently portrayed in terms of limited and unequal access to food, nutrition, health care, educational and job opportunities, and so on. Consequently, political rights tend to be ignored, or at best, receive a second order priority. This is more so the case when some argue, rather benevolently, that what the poor need as a priority are jobs, adequate food, access to basic health services and education, and not so much the right to participation in politics or public decision-making.

The paper examines, first of all, the extent of gender inequality in human capabilities across Indian states, and argues that ensuring a more equal expansion of capabilities, besides being intrinsically significant, can be extremely important for advancing women's well-being. Secondly, it argues that political rights are as important as social and economic rights, and there is no justification for giving primacy to social and economic rights over political rights. Drawing upon the experience of Manipur, the paper seeks to establish that greater political participation and collective action by women are in fact necessary for improving social and economic conditions. Recognizing the importance of enhancing political rights assumes special significance especially as unfortunate scepticism has begun to undermine India's programme of political decentralization.

ASSESSING INEQUALITIES IN HUMAN CAPABILITIES

UNDP's *Human Development Report 1995* proposes the computation of a Gender-related Development Index (GDI) to supplement the Human Development Index (HDI). The GDI concentrates on the same variables as the HDI but focuses on the inequality between men and women as well as on the average achievement of all people taken together. In essence, the GDI is the HDI adjusted for gender inequality.[4]

Table 1 presents basic demographic data as well as the values of HDI and GDI for 16 Indian states. India's GDI value works out to 0.388, and it varies from 0.293 and 0.306 in Uttar Pradesh and Bihar respectively to 0.565 in Kerala. Whereas India as a whole ranks 99th out of 130 countries on the GDI, there are only thirteen countries in the world that record a lower GDI value than Uttar Pradesh and Bihar. That the population of these two states is twice the combined population of the thirteen countries with lower GDI values is indeed a sad commentary on India's development. Kerala has done well on the GDI, and ranks seventy third in the world along with China.

TABLE 1. BASIC DEMOGRAPHIC AND SOCIO-ECONOMIC DATA

State	Population (million) (1)	Female-Male Ratio (2)	Life Expectancy at Birth (Years) (1990-2) (3)	Adult Literacy Rate (%) (4)	Infant Mortality Rate (5)	Total Fertility Rate (6)	Per Capita State Domestic Product (Rs/Year) (1991-2) (7)	Human Development Index (8)	Gender-related Development Index (9)
Andhra Pradesh	67	972	60.3	40.1	69	2.8	5,700	0.400	0.371
Assam	22	923	54.3	49.4	79	3.4	4,230	0.379	0.347
Bihar	86	911	59.4	38.7	71	4.6	2,904	0.354	0.306
Gujarat	41	934	60.2	56.7	64	3.2	6,425	0.467	0.437
Haryana	16	865	62.8	49.9	69	3.8	8,690	0.489	0.370
Himachal Pradesh	5	976	64.0	50.9	68	3.1	5,355	0.454	0.432
Karnataka	45	960	61.8	52.2	72	2.0	5,555	0.448	0.417
Kerala	29	1,036	71.6	86.0	15	1.7	4,618	0.603	0.565
Madhya Pradesh	66	931	53.8	41.8	109	4.4	4,077	0.349	0.312
Maharashtra	79	934	63.9	60.3	56	2.0	8,180	0.523	0.492
Orissa	32	971	55.4	46.4	116	3.1	4,068	0.373	0.329
Punjab	20	882	66.4	51.8	55	3.1	9,643	0.529	0.424
Rajasthan	44	910	57.7	36.1	83	4.5	4,361	0.356	0.309
Tamil Nadu	56	974	62.1	50.6	57	2.2	5,078	0.438	0.402
Uttar Pradesh	139	879	55.8	38.4	96	5.2	4,012	0.348	0.293
West Bengal	68	917	61.2	57.1	65	2.9	5,383	0.459	0.399
India	846	927	59.2	48.7	78	3.6	5,583	0.423	0.388

Sources: Columns 1 and 2 from *Census of India 1991*; Columns 3, 5 and 6 from Sample Registration System; Column 4 are estimates derived from 1991 Census figures of total literacy; Column 7 from *Economic Survey 1994-95*; Columns 8 and 9 from Shiva Kumar (1995).

Note: Female-Male Ratio = number of females per thousand males; IMR = infant deaths/1000 live births; TFR = average number of children expected to be born per woman during her entire reproductive span.

As against an HDI value of 0.423, India's GDI value is 0.388. The two would have been the same if there had been perfect equality between women and men in the formation of human capabilities. The extent of disparity between the HDI and GDI, however, varies across the states. The lowest differentials are to be found in Himachal Pradesh, Maharashtra, and Kerala, and the highest in Haryana and Punjab, two states noted for their high per capita incomes but extremely adverse female-to-male ratios.

EQUALITY, FERTILITY AND GOOD HEALTH

Measuring the health status of any population poses several problems. The information base relating to women's health in particular is very weak. Even the recently conducted National Family Health Survey (1992-3) presents very little data on women's health. The section on 'morbidity and mortality', most directly related to health, has five subsections: (a) morbidity and physical impairments (malaria, partial and complete blindness, physical impairments of the limbs, tuberculosis, and leprosy); (b) crude death rates and aggregate specific death rates; (c) infant and child mortality; (d) high-risk fertility behaviour; and (e) maternal mortality. Morbidity data on women suffer from several problems. It is well known, for instance, that various economic and socio-cultural barriers prevent women from accessing health services. As a result, to the extent that health care centres and hospitals are the main sources of data on morbidity, the information gathered suffers from under-reporting by women. At the same time, the diagnosis of women's health problems may also not be accurate given the inadequacy and even non-availability of sufficiently well-trained and qualified female health professionals. Compounding these problems are also differences in the perceptions of well-being between women and men which influence health-seeking behaviour. In general, it is reported that women in India tend to complain less about ill-health than men. Sen (1985), for instance, reports that in a survey of an equal number of widows and widowers carried out by the All India Institute of Hygiene and Public Health in Singrur near Calcutta during 1944, one year after the Bengal Famine, 48.5 per cent of widowers reported that they were 'ill' or in 'indifferent' health, whereas the proportion of widows who had the same perception was only 2.5 per cent. Interestingly, whereas 46.5 per cent widowers reported as being in the subjective category of 'indifferent' health, the corresponding proportion of widows was zero per cent. Sen (1984) argues that the

> most blatant forms of inequalities and exploitations survive in the world through making allies out of the deprived and the exploited. The underdog learns to bear the burden so well that he or she overlooks the burden itself. Discontent is replaced with acceptance, hopeless rebellion with conformist quiet, and most relevantly in the present context suffering and anger with cheerful endurance.

These comments assume enormous significance especially while undertaking research and interpreting data relating to women's health in India.

Specialized data on women's health, and particularly reproductive health, are extremely limited. Some indication, very indirectly though, can be obtained from Total Fertility Rate (TFR). The TFR gives us the average number of births per woman in a society. The higher the TFR, the greater is the vulnerability and burden faced by women. At the same time, too many births too close together, or at too young or too old an age are a major cause of illness, disability, poor nutrition and premature death among both women and children. To that extent, fewer births can contribute dramatically to improve the lives of women and children in society.

Fertility levels tend to decline with advances in the overall level of human development, and especially with improvements in the levels of female literacy and in the overall position of women in society. Such a relationship holds in the case of Indian states as well, and is captured in the following regression equation:

$$TFR = 7.21 - 8.82 \text{ (HDI)}$$
$$(-3.92)$$
$$R^2 = 0.52; n = 16$$

where:
TFR = Total Fertility Rate
HDI = Human Development Index

Recent discussions concerning fertility behaviour have drawn attention more broadly to women's empowerment, and women's ability to negotiate and exercise control over reproductive decision-making processes. Consequently, efforts to influence fertility behaviour need to focus, not exclusively and principally on women, but ought to involve men as well. The basic premise then is that higher levels of human development and greater equality between women and men are both important for lowering fertility levels. Such a contention is validated by the relationship between TFRs and GDI for 16 Indian states which is captured by the following regression equation:

$$TFR = 48.53 - 52.14 \,(GDI)$$
$$(-4.97)$$
$$R^2 = 0.64; n = 16$$

where:
TFR = Total Fertility Rate
GDI = Gender-related Development Index

The significantly closer association of TFR to GDI than to HDI—reflected in the higher value of R^2—points to the importance of greater gender equality for reducing fertility rates in society.

SOCIO-ECONOMIC FREEDOM, POLITICAL AWARENESS AND GOOD HEALTH: THE CASE OF MANIPUR AND KERALA

Child survival, particularly the under-five mortality rate (U5MR), has gained widespread acceptance as an important index of development. Many aspects of life are reflected in this one statistic including the income of parents, their educational levels, the prevalence of malnutrition and disease, the availability of clean water, the efficiency of the health care system, and above all, the health and status of women. Given that trends in under-five mortality rates parallel those in infant mortality, the IMR serves as a reasonably good surrogate indicator of the health status of a population.

Table 2 presents data on two sets of Indian states: Kerala and Manipur (the low-IMR states or the so-called 'good health' states) and four high-IMR states (or the so-called 'poor health' states): Bihar, Madhya Pradesh, Rajasthan, and Uttar Pradesh.

The infant mortality rates in Kerala (15) and Manipur (22) are strikingly lower than the levels prevailing in the other four high-IMR states. All the states have per capita incomes lower than the national average.[5] What however distinguishes Manipur and Kerala from the other four high-IMR states is the relatively greater degree of freedom that women in these two states enjoy *vis-à-vis* women in the other four states. Some aspects of the greater social and economic freedom that women enjoy can be discerned from data presented in Table 2. The National Family Health Survey (1992-3) reports, for instance, that whereas the singulate mean age at marriage for Indian women was 20 years, the average age at marriage for women was 25 years in Manipur and 22.1 years in Kerala. This is in sharp contrast to Bihar where the average age at marriage for women was only 18 years, and Rajasthan, 18.4 years. Corroborating this is also the fact that whereas, on average, 54 per cent of Indian women between 20 and 24 years of marriage were married before 18 years, the proportion was 14.3 per cent in Manipur and 19.3 per cent in Kerala. These proportions are much lower than Bihar where more than 69 per cent of women in the age group of 20 to 24 years were married before they were 18 years of age. The greater marital freedom that Manipuri women enjoy is reflected in other aspects of social life as well. There is usually no pressure on women for early marriage unlike in many other parts of India. Also, marriages in Manipur are seldom 'arranged' by parents, as is still the dominant tradition in most parts of India; Manipuri women are free to choose their own partners.

Women in Kerala and Manipur also enjoy better access to educational and occupational opportunities. The National Family Health Survey (1992-3) reveals that whereas only 5.2 per cent of girls in the age group of 6 to 14 years in Kerala and 13.2 per cent in Manipur did not attend school, the proportion varied between 45 per cent and 62 per cent in the four high IMR states. That nearly 62 per cent of girls in the age group of 6 to 14 years did not attend school in Bihar is indeed a shocking reflection of the denial of one of the most fundamental rights of any child.

Similarly, women in Manipur also enjoy more freedom to pursue occupations of their choice. The female work participation rate in Manipur (39 per cent) is one of the highest in the country. It is higher than the national average of 22 per cent, and significantly more than the rates reported in Uttar Pradesh (12 per cent) and Bihar (15 per cent). Most of the women are engaged in handloom weaving, petty trade, and other home-based activities that give them some flexibility to combine outside and domestic work. A unique feature of the handloom sector is that all activities, from the procurement of raw materials to the production and marketing of fabric, are undertaken almost exclusively by women, unlike in many other parts of the country where men often operate the loom, and nearly always market the product.[6]

TABLE 2. DEMOGRAPHIC AND SOCIO-ECONOMIC DATA ON 'GOOD' AND 'POOR' HEALTH STATES OF INDIA

State	Population (million) 1991	Female-Male Ratio	Per Capita State Domestic Product (Rs/Year) (1991-2)	Crude Birth Rate 1991-3 (per 1000 Population)	Crude Death Rate 1991-3	Life Expectancy at Birth (Years) (1990-2) F	Life Expectancy at Birth (Years) (1990-2) M	Infant Mortality Rate 1991-3	Literacy Rate Age 7-plus % F	Literacy Rate Age 7-plus % M	Percentage of Girls 6-14 Years Not Attending School
	1	2	3	4	5	6	7	8	9	10	11
Kerala	29	1,036	5,140	17.8	6.1	74.4	68.8	15	86	94	5.2
Manipur	1.8	958	4,653	20.0	5.3	n.a.	n.a.	22	48	72	13.2
Bihar	86	911	2,871	31.7	10.5	58.3	60.4	71	23	52	61.7
Madhya Pradesh	66	931	4,377	34.7	13.1	53.5	54.1	109	29	58	45.2
Rajasthan	44	910	4,511	34.4	9.8	57.8	57.6	83	20	55	59.4
Uttar Pradesh	139	879	3,979	36.0	11.8	54.6	56.8	96	25	56	51.8
India	846	927	5,603	29.0	9.7	59.4	59.0	78	39	64	41.1

Sources: Columns 1 and 2 from *Census of India 1991*; Column 3 from *Economic Survey 1994-5*; Columns 4, 5, 6, 7 and 8 from SRS; Columns 9 and 10 derived from 1991 Census figures of total literacy; and Column 11 from NFHS 1992-3.

Women in Manipur also have a tradition of collective action, organized around the marketplace, and at home. Several informal organizations, locally known as *marups* (friendship association), have been formed by both men and women at the village level.[7] A commonly formed 'friendship association' is the marriage *marup*. When a son or daughter of any member gets married, every member of the association makes a small predetermined contribution to cover part of the marriage expenses. Sometimes, members agree to contribute a fixed amount of money as well as a fixed amount of rice. 'Savings associations' also exist for the purchase of specific commodities, such as brass buckets, bicycles, gold, and so on. While membership of the *marup* is usually open to both men and women, there are also exclusive women's *marups* where members offer wage labour to collect money for the association to be used for different occasions and purposes. There are trade *marups* organized around a common product (example, fish *marup*, rice *marup*, etc.) to provide mutual assistance. Similar *marups* exist to cover funeral costs, and to meet expenses incurred on religious ceremonies and cultural events. Particularly impressive are the informal credit organizations that exist for making consumption and emergency loans.

WOMEN'S POLITICAL ACTION AND GOOD HEALTH IN MANIPUR

An equally striking feature of Manipur and Kerala, the two 'good health' states, is the high rates of political participation by women. Even though Manipuri women have not had adequate representation in formally elected assemblies or in traditional local decision-making bodies, they have played an active role in public life. The dominating role of women in the valley is noticeable in their commanding presence in the marketplace, as well as from their participation, over the years, in a number of agitations against the policies of the state. In 1891, for instance, following a palace revolt, local Manipuris allegedly responsible for the death of five British officers were tried, found guilty and sentenced to be hanged in the Imphal Polo Grounds. Women turned out in large numbers to protest against the sentence by the British. B.C. Allen (1905) describes the scene of the hanging thus:

As far as the eye could see, the plane was white with women. In the Raja's days, a criminal sentenced to death was occasionally reprieved if a sufficient number of women appeared to intercede for him, and hoping that possibly the old custom might still prevail, the women had assembled there in thousands.

The women's agitation of 1939, known locally as Nupi Lan (Women's War), is perhaps the best-known protest by women against the policies of the British. Rice continued to be exported out of the valley during the early part of the twentieth century, but in small quantities. By 1925, however, Marwari traders (non-Manipuris from outside the state) had taken over the entire movement of rice from the valley, and even though exports were permitted only for six weeks, the use of motor vehicles resulted in large outflows. Singh (1991), for instance, reports that around 940 tons of rice were exported out of the state in 1897-8, and this increased to nearly 5,700 tons by 1925-6. After 1925, rice exports continued to increase rapidly, and reached a level of around 13,770 tons by 1938. During this period, the area under rice cultivation increased marginally by about 5 per cent, from 1,75,537 acres in 1925 to 1,85,312 acres in 1938. As a result, the valley began to experience a severe shortage of rice, which was accentuated in 1939 by untimely monsoons that damaged the year's harvest. Marwari traders still continued to buy rice for milling and sale outside the state. The crisis peaked in December, when the local price of rice almost doubled. Nearly a thousand women gathered near the market, and marched in procession to the office of the Political Agent demanding a ban on rice exports, and the closure of all rice mills. Gradually, many more women joined the protest, and soon there were nearly 4,000 women who are reported to have surrounded the British officer, refusing to let him leave the premises until orders banning rice exports were issued. The situation became very tense, and the government called in the army. A clash broke out between the women and the soldiers in which nearly thirty women were injured. The crowds were finally dispersed, but the agitation by women continued until finally the government issued orders banning the export of rice.

Even today, around 2,000 stalls in the main market are owned and managed by women where fruits, vegetables, foodgrains, clothes, and other items of daily consumption are sold. The control over the marketplace has given women a centrality in the economic life of the valley, and an opportunity for collective organization and action. In the mid-1980s, the state government decided to rebuild the marketplace, and plans were made to relocate the women's stalls. The local organization of women traders suspected the government's motives, and for several weeks, launched a 'sit-in' protest. Fearing forcible evacuation, women took turns to stay in the market, and did not vacate the stalls even during the night. At the same time, groups of women actively lobbied with state government officials until the orders for the reconstruction of the marketplace were finally withdrawn.[8]

In the mid-1970s, women in the valley launched a major campaign to prevent sale of liquor and check misbehaviour by drunks. The 'night patrollers of Manipur', as they are referred to, still patrol some of the local areas bearing flaming torches, stopping men and checking for alcohol consumption.[9] More recently, women have taken up the fight against drugs. A newspaper report describes their efforts thus: 'In August, the *numis* [local term for women] held rallies and meetings addressed by top social workers from other parts of India, beat up drug addicts and forced many into rehabilitation centres' (*India Abroad*, 27 September 1991).

Such activism is also reflected in data on voting patterns in national and local elections. Table 3 shows the voter turnout rates in the two sets of states during the tenth Lok Sabha elections of 1991.

Whereas in Kerala, the male and female voter turnout rates were equal and as high as 73 per cent, in Manipur, the female voter turnout rate was 70 per cent, slightly higher than the male voter turnout rate of 69 per cent. In both states, the female turnout rates were distinctly higher than in the four 'poor health' states where the figures ranged from 35 per cent in Rajasthan to 49 per cent in Bihar.

The association between greater political and collective action by women and better health in Manipur and Kerala is not a coincidence. On the contrary, the prominent role played by women has led to a better provisioning of social services in both states. At the same time, it gets favourably translated into much less discrimination against women and girls in society. Several studies in India, for instance, have repeatedly pointed to the strong male bias that exists in the use of health services. Kynch and Sen (1983) found that even urban medical care facilities tended to be used more by men than women, and the differential was particularly large for children. Such differentials were found to be more pronounced in the case of children than adults. Similarly, Sachar *et al.* (1990) found that of those who came as outpatients to the paediatrics departments of two teaching institutions in Ludhiana, 65 per cent were boys and only 35 per cent were girls. Again, boys accounted for 84 per cent of all children admitted as in-patients in the hospitals, and girls for only 16 per cent. This does not necessarily suggest that boys are less healthy than girls, but that son preference gets translated into boys receiving better and more prompt medical attention than girls. The same study also reports that a higher proportion of girls admitted as in-patients

TABLE 3. TENTH LOK SABHA ELECTIONS, 1991: FEMALE AND MALE TURNOUT RATES

State	Female Turnout Rate (%)	Male Turnout Rate (%)	Ratio of Female-Male Turnout Rate
Kerala	73	73	1.00
Manipur	70	69	1.01
Bihar	49	70	0.70
Madhya Pradesh	35	53	0.66
Rajasthan	39	54	0.72
Uttar Pradesh	44	51	0.86
India	51	62	0.82

Source: Computed from Election Commissioner's reports, Government of India.

died compared to boys, suggesting that even the fewer number of girls who were admitted were brought late during the course of their illness.

An interesting counter-example, however, was found in data collected from the Regional Medical College Hospital in Imphal. Between 1985 and 1990, more adult women outpatients (including obstetric and gynaelcological cases) visited the hospital than men. When obstetric and gynaecological cases were excluded, the male-to-female ratio of outpatients was found to be favourable to men, though there was a steady improvement (favouring women) over the five-year period (See Figures 1 and 2).

At the same time, the percentage of in-patients who died was lower for adult female than for male in-patients, while no such pattern was found in the case of children. One needs to interpret such hospital-based data with extreme caution. But the patterns seem to suggest that the extent of gender bias in the use of health services is much less in situations where women enjoy greater freedom.[10]

CONCLUDING REMARKS

This paper examines, *first* of all, the extent of gender inequality in human capabilities across sixteen Indian states, and argues that ensuring a more equal expansion of capabilities must become a national priority. That there are only thirteen countries in the world with a lower value of GDI than Uttar Pradesh and Bihar is a national shame, and that twice as many people live in these two states than in the thirteen countries with lower GDI is a sad reflection of the state of social progress in the

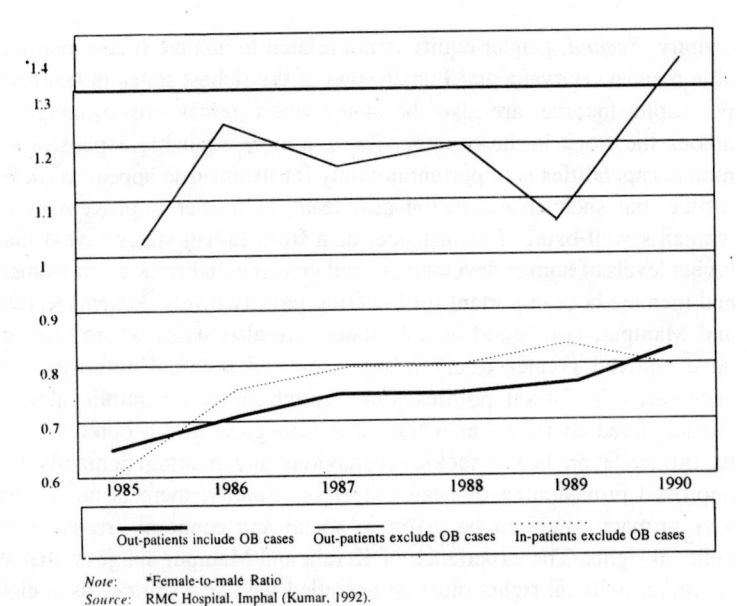

FIGURE 1. FEMALE-TO-MALE RATIO OF ADULT IN-PATIENTS AND OUT-PATIENTS

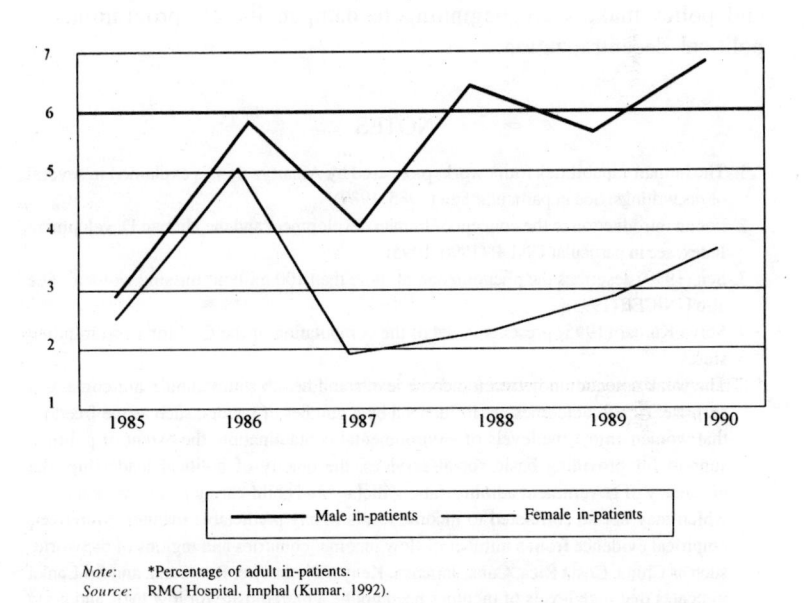

FIGURE 2. PERCENTAGE OF ADULT IN-PATIENTS WHO DIED IN RMC HOSPITAL, IMPHAL

country. *Second*, gender equity is not related to income in any predictable manner. Haryana and Punjab, two of the richest states in terms of per capita income, are also the states where female disadvantage is among the worst in the country. *Third*, a more equitable expansion of human capabilities is important not only for its intrinsic appeal to social justice, but such an expansion also leads to further improvement in women's well-being. For instance, data from Indian states reveal that higher levels of human development and greater equality between women and men are both important for lowering fertility levels. *Fourth*, Kerala and Manipur, two 'good health' states, are also states where women have enjoyed greater freedom and exercised political authority not necessarily in formal politics, but through collective public action. Greater freedom for women translates into good health outcomes by its influence on health-seeking behaviour and making demands for improved provisioning of health services. *Finally*, there is no reason why primacy ought to be given to social and economic rights over political rights. The experience of Kerala and Manipur suggests that if anything, political rights must be accorded the same priority as socioeconomic rights if human development gains have to be maximized and sustained. Such a recognition is critical for India's development especially now as cynicism and scepticism among some public administrators and policy-makers are beginning to dampen India's programme of political decentralization.

NOTES

1. The human capabilities framework, pioneered by Amartya Sen, is explained in several of his writings. See in particular Sen (1985, 1989).
2. For an introduction to the concept of human development and the Human Development Index, see in particular UNDP (1990, 1995).
3. Sen (1990) describes the phenomenon of more than 100 million 'missing women'. See also UNICEF (1995).
4. Shiva Kumar (1995) presents in detail the computation of the GDI for sixteen Indian states.
5. The weak association between income levels and health status should not come as a surprise. Health outcomes are influenced by a number of factors, such as the freedom that women enjoy, the levels of environmental contamination, the extent of political support for providing basic social services, the quality of political leadership, the efficiency of government administration, dietary and child-caring practices, and so on which may not be correlated to income levels in any predictable manner. Moreover, empirical evidence from a number of 'low income' countries and regions of the world, such as China, Costa Rica, Cuba, Jamaica, Kenya, Zimbabwe, Botswana, and Sri Lanka indicates that high levels of incomes need not be a prerequisite for low IMR and good

health. In these countries and regions, governments with a strong political commitment to social development, and a mix of appropriate policy interventions in the health sector, have been able to record impressive gains in health and welfare indicators. See also Caldwell (1986), Dreze and Sen (1995) and Rockefeller Foundation (1985).

6. The phenomenon of high levels of women's participation in the 'economic' activities of Manipur is not new, but was noted even at the turn of the century. Allen (1905), for instance, wrote:

> Women exceed men in numbers. They enjoy a position of considerable importance, and most of the trade of the valley is in their hands. ... The internal trade of the state is carried on at markets which are held in the neighbourhood of the larger villages. ... Almost all the business is transacted by women, who are shrewd and capable, the men thinking it below their dignity to come and traffic at the bazaar. ...

7. Chaki-Sircar (1984) describes the functioning of several of these *marups*; the examples cited here draw on her case studies.
8. Eyewitness account of Vina Mazumdar.
9. See Jain (1980) for a detailed account of the women's efforts to curb alcohol sale and consumption in the valley.
10. Many of these features of Manipur that suggest greater freedom for women should not be taken to imply that there is no discrimination against women. Both in the valley and in the hills, communities are essentially patriarchal and patrilineal. Among the scheduled tribe population, no share of the immovable property is inherited by daughters. In case there are no sons in the family, immovable property goes to the brothers of the deceased, though movable property is distributed among women. There are food and other taboos that apply exclusively to women. While women's rights to maintenance are recognized, these are conditional.

REFERENCES

Allen, B.C., 1905. *Naga Hills and Manipur: Socio-economic History*, Gian Publications, Delhi (reprinted 1980).

Anand, Sudhir and Amartya Sen, 1995. 'Gender Inequality in Human Development: Theories and Measurement', *Human Development Report Office Occasional Paper 19*, UNDP, New York.

Caldwell, John C., 1986. 'Routes to Low Mortality in Poor Countries', *Population and Development Review* 12(2).

Chaki-Sircar, Manjusri, 1984. *Feminism in a Traditional Society: Women of the Manipur Valley*, Vikas, New Delhi.

Dreze, Jean, 1989. *Hunger and Public Action*, Oxford University Press, New Delhi.

────── and Sen, Amartya, 1995. *India: Economic Development and Social Opportunity*, Oxford University Press, New Delhi.

Government of India, 1992. 'Final Population Totals: Brief Analysis of Primary Census Abstract', Paper 2 of 1992, Registrar General and Gensus Commissioner, New Delhi.

──────, 1993. *Education for All: The Indian Scene*, Department of Education, New Delhi.

──────, 1995. *Economic Survey 1994-95*, Ministry of Finance, New Delhi.

International Institute for Population Sciences, 1994. *National Family Health Survey (1992-93)*, Bombay.

Jain, Devaki, 1980. 'The Night Patrollers of Manipur', in Devaki Jain *et al.*, *Women's Quest for Power: Five Indian Case Studies*, Vikas, New Delhi.

Kumar, A.K. Shiva, 1991. 'UNDP's Human Development Index: A Computation for Indian States', *Economic and Political Weekly* 26(41).

————, 1992. 'Maternal Capabilities and Child Survival in Low Income Region: An Economic Analysis of Infant Mortality in India', Ph.D. Dissertation, Harvard University (unpublished).

————, 1995. 'UNDP's Gender-related Development Index: A Computation for Indian States', *Economic and Political Weekly* 31(14), 16 April.

Kynch, Jocelyn and Amartya Sen, 1983. 'Indian Women: Well-Being and Survival', *Cambridge Journal of Economics* 7.

Lal Dena (ed.), 1991. *History of Modern Manipur (1826-1949)*, Orbit Publishers, New Delhi.

Rockefeller Foundation, 1985. *Good Health at Low Cost*, Rockefeller Foundation, New York.

Sachar, R.K., J. Verma, S. Dhawan, Ved Prakash, A. Chopra and R. Adalka, 1990. 'Sex Bias in Health and Medical Care Allocation', *Indian Journal of Medical and Child Health* 1(2).

Sen, Amartya, 1984. 'Goods and People' in idem, *Resources, Values and Development*, Harvard University Press, Cambridge, Mass.

————, 1985. *Commodities and Capabilities*, Oxford University Press, Delhi.

————, 1989. 'Development as Capability Expansion', in Human Development in the 1980s and Beyond, *Journal of Development Planning*, United Nations, No. 19.

————, 1990. 'More than 100 million Women are Missing', *New York Review of Books*, 20 December.

Singh, Joykumar N., 1991. 'Women's Agitation of 1939', in Lal Dena (ed.).

UNDP, 1990. *Human Development Report 1990*, Oxford University Press, New York.

————, 1995. *Human Development Report 1995*, Oxford University Press, New York.

UNICEF, 1995. *The Progress of Indian States*, India Country Office, New Delhi.

Vaidyanathan, A., 1994. 'Employment Situation: Some Emerging Perspectives', *Economic and Political Weekly* 29(50).

II
Micro Studies on Gender and Reproduction

Poverty, Gender Inequality and Reproductive Choice: Some Findings from a Household Survey in U.P.

SWAPNA MUKHOPADHYAY
PRAACHI TEWARI GANDHI
R. SAVITHRI

In this paper an attempt has been made to delineate the overlap between poverty, gender inequality and reproductive choice as manifested through observed fertility behaviour, using household survey data from five districts of rural Uttar Pradesh.[1] Much of the recent demographic literature in India and abroad has sought to explain fertility behaviour through changes in women's status. This paper seeks to add to the existing knowledge based on the complex linkages between gender inequality, poverty and reproductive behaviour. In doing so, we have also explored the contrasts between men's and women's reproductive roles and motivations. Often it is implicitly assumed—with little empirical data to support the assumption—that fertility decisions are made by the couple as a unit and that male and female attitudes towards child-bearing are not dissimilar. Our paper makes an attempt to study not only fertility behaviour as based on women's motivations for having children, their knowledge and use of contraception, etc., but also focuses on how family partnerships are played out when men's and women's desires do not coincide. A key barrier to the realization of a woman's reproductive choice is her inability to overcome disagreements within her own household. All this has at its base the wider social and historical context of gender bias. A discussion on reproductive choice must confront this reality and address women's needs, not merely through education and better livelihood options, but also through empowerment in interpersonal dealings with the husband and members of her extended family.

Sociological and anthropological research on women suggest that, generally, Indian women enjoy little autonomy. Family decisions relating to finances, etc., even selection of mates are generally made by men

(Jeffrey et al. 1989). Marriage practices such as village exogamy, patrilocal residence, patrilineal inheritance patterns, women's low and infrequent contact with their natal kin, etc., also tend to make Indian women powerless, and physically and socially secluded (Altekar 1959; Karve 1965). The consequent low status of women also undermines demographic decision-making. The pace of demographic change has been the slowest in the Hindi-speaking region of India. Demographic transition theories seek to link changes in demographic variables such as rates of fertility and mortality, primarily, with levels of economic development. It is, however, now accepted that very disparate stages of demographic transition may be associated with similar levels of economic development.[2] Thus, per capita incomes in Kerala and Uttar Pradesh are not too dissimilar, while fertility-mortality rates are drastically so. Female literacy and women's involvement in the labour market are also pointed out as factors explaining differences in fertility patterns.[3] Female literacy variable is now accepted as perhaps the single most important variable affecting fertility; the impact of women's involvement in the labour market being more ambiguous. Our results suggest, however, that a great deal depends upon the context. Even if groups of women have markedly different ability to read and write, it may not be reflected in different levels of awareness or status if their cultural milieu is unvarying within the sample. Work participation *per se* may also be a misleading indicator of autonomy, especially under conditions of dire poverty. In other words, a hypothesis which may have been vindicated by countrywide cross-sectional data, may stand rejected by data from a relatively homogeneous cultural region. A variable may come up with explanatory power on a macro scale, but in a region-specific study, its explanatory power may become doubtful, if the data show limited variability.

ISSUES AND HYPOTHESES

For this study, a few indices of poverty and gender inequality were chosen to consider their impact on male and female reproductive behaviour and choices. Reproductive choice has been measured by fertility indices such as number of pregnancies, number of live births and actual reporting of contraceptive use. While there are many unseen linkages between actual outcomes and the parameters of choice, the options available to a woman are hard to map using survey data.

The chosen indicators have their limitations. For example, for number of pregnancies, no distinction has been made between wanted and unwanted pregnancies. Survey data also do not give total fertility rates for different age groups. Although one can calculate age-adjusted fertility rates, this has not been attempted here. Contraceptive use is a better indicator of choice, but tells us no more than whether or not a particular woman wants to control fertility.

The main purpose of the paper has been to see whether poverty and gender inequality have a significant impact on fertility behaviour and reproductive choice. An attempt has also been made alongside to test various existing hypotheses on fertility patterns and contraceptive use. Poverty has been measured by per capita household income and size of landholding. Gender discrimination is seen to be manifested through differences in male and female literacy levels, female labour force participation rates and other socio-cultural variables. Other indicators considered are the woman's say in spending household income and deciding on the family size, the difference in husband-wife perceptions on the schooling of male *vis-à-vis* female children, and the number of sons and daughters desired, etc. Certain other variables which are considered important in determining reproductive choice are child mortality, socio-cultural variables such as caste, purdah, age at marriage for men and women, age at *gauna*, and so on.

Recent research on demographic change has identified a number of possible relationships between reproductive behaviour/choice on the one hand, and variables such as poverty and gender inequality on the other. As the World Bank country study (1991) points out, the study of poverty is primarily 'the study of access and of constraints to access'. Poverty denies access to health, in terms of status and services. And health is a crucial link between poverty and reproductive choice.

Poverty affects, both preventive and curative aspects of health. At the preventive level the poor have inadequate ability to acquire a nutritious diet, better living and working conditions and other attendant factors that would prevent ill-health. The result is endemic occurrence of communicable diseases and diseases related to deficient nutrition. At the same time, health care services available to the poor in terms of physical accessibility, monetary cost and effectiveness are minimal.[4] The negative effect of poverty on women's health is even more acute because of the existing gender bias against women. Gender bias in nutrition and health care in childhood, early marriage and conception, lack of voluntary check on the family size and poor state of pre-natal and maternal health care services only intensify women's health problems.

Further, as Ravindran (1993) argues, women's poor health status through various intervening variables affects their reproductive choice.

Poor health leads, for example, to a high incidence of wasted pregnancies and secondary infertility. This is an important reason why women do not want to voluntarily limit their family size. Also, poor living conditions and other factors increase infant mortality rate (IMR), and wherever IMR is high, couples are reluctant to limit their family size. Poverty also leads to the belief that more mouths to feed also mean twice the number of hands to work. Thus, children are considered as economic assets and the greater the number of children greater the sense of security. Environmental degradation makes fuel wood gathering, livestock pasturing and water fetching more difficult (World Bank, 1992). As these are tasks that children can do, the value of children increases for parents. And these links are strongest where female fertility is already high.

Poverty also indirectly denies access to contraceptive knowledge and methods to an impoverished woman even if she is inclined to limit her family. The limited income of the household does not allow her to take a day off in order to access information on contraceptive methods from the local primary health care centre or undergo sterilization. However some of the scholars such as Miller (1981, 1993) and Krishnaji (1987) have argued, poverty is correlated with less female discrimination and, thus, may positively influence reproductive choice.

The most commonly used yardstick for measuring poverty is income, which also, to some extent, indicates consumption patterns. Several other aspects related to poverty such as access to education, health care services and general living conditions are not directly included. The poverty line is defined mainly in terms of income required for a certain minimum amount of calorie intake. Survey data can be useful in broadening this definition.

Not much research is there on the direct links between gender discrimination and reproductive choice in India. There is need to put the question of gender bias and gender relations at the centre of issues relating to reproductive health and rights, policies and programmes to empower women, and to motivate men to take responsibility for reproductive matters (Germain *et al.* 1994). Indian women's reproductive and marital choices are particularly limited by their social and economic circumstances. It is important not to assume that individuals make decisions in a vacuum or that everybody makes 'choices' equally 'freely'. Due to existing social inequalities, the resources and range of options available to women differ greatly, affecting their ability to exercise their rights (Williams 1991).

The realm of sexual and reproductive decisions and rights are embedded in the social matrix and the process of socialization through which individuals imbibe the power of decision-making. Gender bias starts within the family, making a far-reaching impact on demographic outcomes. Discrimination against daughters in access to food and health care, early marriage, repeated pregnancies and high prevalence of son preference perpetuate a cycle of ideology and consequent actions. The difference in the way boys and girls are socialized within the family influences differences in men's and women's decision-making capacities. We have selected for consideration a few such variables as determinants of reproductive behaviour and choice. These are:

— Male and female education and reproductive behaviour and decision-making;
— Women's work and reproductive behaviour; and
— Cultural aspects affecting reproductive behaviour.

EDUCATION AND REPRODUCTIVE DECISION-MAKING

A number of studies provide evidence of a strong correlation between women's educational level and a couple's fertility (Cleland and Rodriguez 1988; Cochrane 1979).

World Fertility Survey data also indicate strong associations between women's education and age at marriage, desired family size and contraceptive use in developing countries (United Nations 1987). Some studies have attempted to assess how education may influence women's personal attitudes and their role in decision-making. It is found, for instance, that education not only delays the wife's age at marriage but also increases husband-wife communication and knowledge, and improves attitudes and access to birth control—all of which are negatively related to fertility. It is less clear, however, whether it is only a woman's formal education that is a primary determinant of her contraceptive knowledge (Dixon 1993). Most studies assess the easily quantifiable years of schooling, but do not address such other forms of training as adult literacy programmes, informal education and exposure to extension services, which are more difficult to measure.

Mahmud and Johnston (1994), who have presented their findings in this regard, also point out that it is possible that the effective use of birth control and choice as to number of children could depend on the woman's attitude towards, experience of, and knowledge about family planning and health services, irrespective of whether she has ever attended formal school. Other sources besides formal schooling, such as peer and support networks, woman's assets in terms of property and savings, her autonomy in matters related to affairs at home and outside, and informal education may be even more important for which further research needs to be done.

WOMEN'S WORK AND REPRODUCTIVE BEHAVIOUR

It is widely presumed that women's productivity and participation in the labour force have a positive effect on their health and that of their children. By increasing women's autonomy in the household, as well as financial capacity which leads to less dependence on others, alternative sources of social identity and support increase women's desire to delay marriage, and space or limit births (Dixon 1978; Safilios-Rothschild 1982). There is a caveat, however. The influence of women's economic activity on their reproductive decision-making depends largely on the value placed on women's labour in a particular society and the conditions under which women engage in economic activity. In India, at the lower income levels, a household gains status by withdrawing its women from the labour force. Youssef (1982) suggests that the impact of women's non-domestic work on fertility differs by type of activity and occupation but there has been little consistency in either the strength or the direction of the observed relationship. It has also been suggested that where women take up market employment for want of money, they continue to bear the burden of housework and in such cases, women's employment does not do much to strengthen their capabilities to implement their reproductive preferences (Bruce and Dwyer 1988). In some contexts, it has been found that independent earning by poor women does appear to affect traditional gender relations within the household, enhancing women's participation and say in decisions. Also, those who earn independently appear to exercise a higher degree of autonomy, as shown by their higher use of birth control and significantly greater physical mobility (Mahmud 1993; Nelson 1979). There is maximum benefit when women directly control the income they earn and such women were found to limit births (Mahmud 1993).

It is seen, therefore, that the relationship between gainful employment and greater reproductive and sexual choice depend on a large number of factors such as type of occupation, income, motivation, labour status, and terms and conditions of employment.

CULTURAL FACTORS AFFECTING REPRODUCTIVE BEHAVIOUR

Amongst the cultural factors affecting reproductive behaviour and decision-making an important one is the concept of female autonomy. Female autonomy refers to woman's ability to take decisions on her own, without requiring others' permission in matters ranging from her decision to work, to retain her income, how to spend household income, what to cook, where to go, etc. For the purpose of analysis of the data at hand, indices of dimensions of female autonomy were constructed as follows:

Economic autonomy. Women were questioned on a set of issues including:

— Independent source of income (if any);
— Who retained the money earned by women (husband or other members of the family);
— Whether women received any money for household expenses; and
— Whether women could buy things (clothes etc.) for themselves without the permission of husband or other members of their marital household.

Combinations of these questions were chosen to arrive at an index of women with 'no' economic autonomy, 'middle level' economic autonomy, 'low' economic autonomy and 'high' economic autonomy.

Personal autonomy. An index was constructed for personal autonomy in similar manner using information on factors such as restrictions on mobility, nature of permissible linkages with natal home, etc. (For details see ISST, 1996.)

Marriage and purdah. The other cultural factors mediated by gender that constrain women's choices are related to marriage and purdah. The universality of marriage and the early age at marriage, in the Indian context, makes it difficult for women to have a say in the number and spacing of her children. On the other hand, purdah could imply lower status and limited physical autonomy for women, which is also indicative of low autonomy in all other spheres. These are some of the autonomy indices used to explain variations in reproductive behaviour of women (ISST, 1996).

THE SURVEY

The study was conducted in five districts in Uttar Pradesh and four districts in Karnataka. Districts were chosen to represent different agroclimatic regions within each state (ISST, 1996). In Uttar Pradesh, the districts selected were Almora, Faizabad, Ghazipur, Mathura and Muzaffarnagar, and in Karnataka, Bidar, Dakshina Kannada, Kodagu, Kolar and Mysore. Field work was carried out in 35 villages of Uttar Pradesh and the same number in Karnataka averaging 7-9 villages per district. For the purpose of this paper only the Uttar Pradesh data set has been analysed.

SAMPLE

The total sample size from Uttar Pradesh comprised 1,078 households spread over 35 villages in five districts. The sampled households are predominantly Hindu (87.2 per cent). About 11.5 per cent are Muslims, Christians and others making up the remaining 1.3 per cent. This study is restricted to women in the reproductive age group of 15-49 years and to men with wives in this age group.

Of the total households 21 per cent belong to 'scheduled castes', 21 per cent to 'other backward castes', 7 per cent to scheduled tribes, and 33.4 per cent to 'others'. Respondent households who refused to state their caste constituted 23 per cent.

The monthly household income is less than Rs 850 for nearly 47 per cent of the households, and between Rs 850 and Rs 1,650 for another 30 per cent. Only 10 per cent earn above Rs 2,500 per month. With an average household size of about 6, this places a large majority of the sampled population below the poverty line.

About 98.5 per cent of the sample own houses, though 41.8 per cent have *kutcha* type of house and 50 per cent have one or two rooms in the house. There is no electricity in 80 per cent of the houses. 95 per cent of the sample claimed that sources of water are available within 15 minutes of walking distance, though in summer water is less easily available.

Cultivable land is owned by 74.1 per cent of the sample households. Among them, 13.3 per cent own unirrigated land. Nearly 50 per cent are marginal land owners with 2.5 acres or less of irrigated land.

The occupational structure of adult males suggests that nearly 50 per cent are dependent on agriculture, 10.5 per cent are small traders or do petty business, and 14.35 per cent make up non-agricultural labour.

The survey does not provide adequate indicators for separating out women's involvement in economically productive home-based activities. Nearly 82.5 per cent of the women reported being housewives and involved in home-based work (categories that are clubbed together). While 12 per cent work as agricultural labourers, another 1.8 per cent are reportedly engaged in trade, animal husbandry and other self-employment activities.

Literacy levels are low with 41 per cent of the males and 76 per cent of the females being illiterate. About 8 per cent males and 5.1 per cent females reported to have had some schooling but not completed the primary level, 23.1 per cent of the males and 4.9 per cent of the females surveyed have completed secondary school and above. In 37 per cent cases, the couples are educated to the same level. In 4 per cent cases wives are better educated whereas in nearly 60 per cent cases the husbands have a better educational level. Level of exposure to different mass media such as newspaper, TV or radio is low. Among both men and women, exposure to radio (70 per cent and 36 per cent respectively) is higher than to TV (50 per cent and 23 per cent respectively). Women's exposure is much lower to any of the media.

Both male and female respondents wished to have more sons than daughters. Around 57 per cent wish to have one, two or three more sons, but only 23 per cent wished to have one more daughter; the number wanting more than one daughter was negligible.

The disparity between the male and female child is also apparent in ideas about children's education. Among the female respondents 61 per cent prioritized son's education as compared to 40 per cent males. About 30 per cent of the females and 47 per cent males wished to give equal importance to son's and daughter's education. The number prioritizing daughter's education was negligible.

Inheritance of family land is seen as the right of sons by nearly 95 per cent of both male and female respondents, the inheritance going to wives and daughters only where there are no sons. In 85 per cent cases, men and women consider that sons are the major source of support in old age in financial and other ways; though for short-term support such as care during illness and economic support during crises, daughters are also counted upon.

Questions were asked of both men and women to elicit information on the prevailing perceptions on women's autonomy and norms of wifely behaviour. In deciding whether women can go out to work, according to men, in 93 per cent cases husbands have a say, and in 65 per cent cases wives have a say. According to women, in 89 per cent cases husbands have a say and in 81 per cent cases wives have a say in the matter. About

85 per cent of the couples sometimes discuss household expenditure issues and 35.5 per cent frequently discuss it.

According to 81.5 per cent men, their wives have a say in spending income, but only 65.3 per cent women consider that they have a say in the matter. The number who expressed they do not have a say is not insignificant whether we consider the responses of males or females.

In 65.5 per cent cases, men and women said that the women did not need family elders' permission to spend money for personal use. Among the 15 per cent households where the women earn money, 50 per cent of the men say that the wives give them their income, but only 25.5 per cent of the women say that they give their income to the husbands.

The contraceptive prevalence rate (CPR), including terminal methods is about 32 per cent.

Around 68 per cent of the couples discuss contraception sometimes, and 7 per cent discuss it frequently. According to 58 per cent of the women a woman decides about contraceptive use together with her spouse; in 23 per cent cases the woman decides; and in 8 per cent cases the husband decides. According to 60 per cent of the men the couple decide together; in 33 per cent cases only the men decide; and in 5 per cent cases only the wives decide.

In 85 per cent cases, couples 'sometimes' discuss how many children to have. Among the male respondents 23 per cent said that the couples 'frequently' discussed the number of children they wished to have; only 13 per cent of the female respondents said there were 'frequent' discussions.

About 65 per cent couples want more children; around 35 per cent consider that the birth of more children depends 'on God'. In most cases, the respondents wish to have one to three more sons and one more daughter.

According to 92 per cent of the men, in their household the husband and wife have the maximum say on how many children to have; a similar response was given by 82 per cent of the women. As regards the elders' say in the matter, male opinion is of greater influence than of the females in 83 per cent cases.

BIVARIATE ANALYSIS: SOME RESULTS

Bivariate tables (refer Tables 1-9) were generated that looked at the distribution of the number of pregnancies and contraceptive use with several variables that are indicators of gender inequality and poverty.

The first limitation of an analysis of bivariate relationships is that it brings to light relationships only between any two individual variables, and therefore, cannot reveal the simultaneous impact of other variables on the chosen 'dependent' variable. This limitation must be borne in mind while interpreting the cross tabulations. However, some of the variables that we discuss below have also been used in multiple regressions, results of which are reported below.

Among Hindus, the scheduled castes and other backward classes show relatively fewer contraceptive users (the difference is about 6 per cent) than the other (higher) castes. The correlation in their case might be a function of the other attendant factors such as poverty or lack of education. A brief mention may also be made of the relation of purdah or *ghunghat* with contraceptive use. Purdah is widespread among Muslims and Hindus in north India. Remarkably, couples where the women practise purdah are using contraceptives in a larger number (37 per cent) than those who do not practise it (26 per cent). While the practice is indicative of a certain lack of freedom for women in present times, it might be continuing without any loss to women's autonomy in so far as it is reflected is contraceptive use!

Contraceptive use also appears to be positively correlated with higher male and female age at marriage. In the two age classes where most women get married, contraceptive use is higher for those getting married between 15 and 20 years than those getting married between 11 and 15 years by about 8 per cent. Similarly, the use of contraceptives for men married between 21 and 25 years is higher than those married between 15 and 20 years (difference more than 10 per cent). Higher age at marriage might imply greater decision-making authority of the woman within the household. Also, late age at marriage may indicate that the couple is better informed in matters such as family planning than those marrying very early. Age at *gauna*, on the other hand, seems to have little effect on contraceptive use, perhaps because it is determined by the onset of puberty that is more 'natural' than 'cultural'.

Decisions related to planning the family size are influenced by the values that socialization inculcates in a person. If one agency of socialization is the family, the other is formal education. Literature on the subject argues that the higher the education of the female, the lower is her fertility. This probably indicates that she has greater choice in relation to restricting reproduction. The sample consists primarily of illiterate women, and therefore, it is difficult to examine the correlation between education and contraceptive use. Men's education is, however,

TABLE 1. EDUCATION LEVEL OF MALE RESPONDENT BY CONTRACEPTIVE USE

Education	Current Contraceptive Use			Total	(%)
	Using	Not Using	No Response/ Do not Know		
Uneducated	39	120	23	182	(34.4)
Less than Primary	15	24	5	44	(8.3)
Primary	24	37	5	66	(12.5)
Middle	37	49	8	94	(17.8)
Matric	26	37	8	71	(13.4)
Higher Secondary	18	25	6	49	(9.3)
Graduation	16	7	-	23	(4.3)
Total	175	299	55	529	
	(33.1)	(56.5)	(10.4)		(100.0)

TABLE 2. EDUCATION LEVEL OF FEMALE RESPONDENT BY CONTRACEPTIVE USE

Education	Current Contraceptive Use			Total	(%)
	Using	Not Using	No Response/ Do not Know		
Uneducated	117	260	25	402	(76.0)
Less than Primary	11	21	2	34	(6.4)
Primary	14	27	7	48	(9.1)
Middle	10	11	-	21	(4.0)
Matric	5	9	2	16	(3.0)
Higher Secondary	3	1	-	4	(0.8)
Graduation	2	1	-	3	(0.6)
No Response/Don't know	-	1	-	1	(0.2)
Total	162	331	36	529	
	(30.6)	(62.6)	(6.8)		(100.0)

found to be positively correlated with contraceptive use. Though contraceptive use is higher for all levels of education in men than illiterate men, the extent of use nearly doubles among couples where the men are graduates. Since in a majority of the cases the women are illiterate, this reveals that men's education does affect reproductive choice for the couple.

The other aspect of a woman's socio-economic status that is believed to give her greater autonomy is her engagement in economically remunerative activity. In our sample, number of women earning independently

TABLE 3. OCCUPATION OF FEMALE RESPONDENT BY CONTRACEPTIVE USE

Occupation	Using	Not Using	No Response/ Do not Know	Total	(%)
Farmer	31	20	3	54	(10.2)
Agricultural Labour	1	10	1	12	(2.3)
Small Trade	-	1	-	1	(0.2)
Unemployed	-	3	-	3	(0.6)
Home Based Work/ Housewife	127	290	32	449	(84.9)
Student	3	2	-	5	(0.9)
Children	-	2	-	2	(0.4)
Others	-	1	-	1	(0.2)
No Response/Don't Know	-	2	-	2	(0.4)
Total	162	331	36	529	
	(30.6)	(62.6)	(6.8)		(100.0)

TABLE 4. WIFE'S SAY IN SPENDING FAMILY INCOME BY CONTRACEPTIVE USE

Wife's Say in Spending Family Income	Using	Not Using	No Response/ Do not Know	Total	(%)
Has a say	112	205	19	336	(63.5)
Does not have say	49	125	19	193	(36.5)
Total	161	330	38	529	
	(30.4)	(62.4)	(7.2)		(100.0)

are very few, which makes analysis of the effect on contraceptive use unclear. There is, in fact, a slight negative correlation, so that contraceptive use declines in families where the woman earns. A woman's independent earning might not, however, necessarily indicate her greater autonomy, and might be due to poverty, and thus does not positively affect contraceptive use. The significance of land owned by the female cannot be ascertained because there are hardly any women in the sample who own land.

Woman's control over household income could mean that she has greater decision-making authority with respect to family size. But in the sample, it is found that say in spending household income, or getting

TABLE 5. WHETHER WIFE IS GIVEN CASH FOR HOUSEHOLD EXPENSE BY CONTRACEPTIVE USE

Cash Given for Household Expenses	Current Contraceptive Use				
	Using	Not Using	No Response/ Do Not Know	Total	(%)
Yes	99	192	19	310	(58.6)
No	63	139	17	219	(41.4)
Total	162	331	36	529	
	(30.6)	(62.6)	(6.8)		(100.0)

TABLE 6A. WHETHER WIFE HAS A SAY IN WORKING OUTSIDE HOME BY CONTRACEPTIVE USE AS ANSWERED BY FEMALE RESPONDENT

Wife's Say	Current Contraceptive Use				
	Using	Not Using	No Response/ Do Not Know	Total	(%)
Wife has no say	47	46	7	100	(18.9)
Wife has say	115	285	29	429	(81.1)
Total	162	331	36	529	
	(30.6)	(62.6)	(6.8)		(100.0)

TABLE 6B. WHETHER WIFE HAS A SAY IN WORKING OUTSIDE HOME BY CONTRACEPTIVE USE AS ANSWERED BY MALE RESPONDENT

Wife's Say	Current Contraceptive Use				
	Using	Not Using	No Response/ Do not Know	Total	(%)
Wife has no say	74	96	17	187	(35.3)
Wife has say	101	203	38	342	(64.7)
Total	175	299	55	529	
	(33.1)	(56.5)	(10.4)		(100.0)

cash in hand for household or personal expenditure has little positive correlation with contraceptive use. In fact, greater freedom to purchase items of personal use is correlated with lower contraceptive use. One reason for this might be that greater autonomy in expenditure does not necessarily mean that the woman would consciously reduce her fertility

TABLE 7A. NUMBER OF MORE SONS WANTED BY CONTRACEPTIVE USE
AS ANSWERED BY FEMALE RESPONDENTS

No. of More Sons Wanted	Using	Not Using	No Response/ Do Not Know	Total	(%)
0	146	195	11	352	(66.6)
1	9	38	6	53	(10.0)
2	5	39	6	50	(9.5)
3	-	4	-	4	(0.8)
On God	2	54	13	69	(13.0)
Unsure	-	1	-	1	(0.2)
Total	162	331	36	529	
	(30.6)	(62.6)	(6.8)		(100.0)

TABLE 7B. NUMBER OF MORE SONS WANTED BY CONTRACEPTIVE USE
AS ANSWERED BY MALE RESPONDENTS

No. of More Sons Wanted	Using	Not Using	No Response/ Do Not Know	Total	(%)
0	150	175	24	349	(66.0)
1	16	35	9	60	(11.3)
2	4	21	9	34	(6.4)
3	-	5	2	7	(1.3)
4	-	1	-	1	(0.2)
On God	3	58	10	71	(13.4)
Unsure	2	4	1	7	(1.3)
Total	175	299	55	529	
	(33.1)	(56.5)	(10.4)		(100.0)

or that she will have the freedom to do so. It is observed, however, that in the few cases where women earn independently, contraceptive use increases where the woman has greater control over her income.

Indicators of women's decision-making authority in relation to working outside home, family size and children's education are not correlated with higher contraceptive use. This might be because of constraints on her decision-making when located in the context of the authority structure in the household. Thus, her say in different matters may not be very important though most women claim to have some say. Further,

TABLE 8. INFANT MORTALITY BY CONTRACEPTIVE USE

Infant Mortality	Current Contraceptive Use				
	Using	Not Using	No Response/ Do not Know	Total	(%)
0	122	218	25	365	(68.8)
1	27	75	9	111	(20.98)
2	6	22	1	29	(5.48)
3	4	8	1	13	(2.5)
4	2	4	-	6	(1.1)
5	-	2	-	2	(0.37)
6	-	2	-	2	(0.37)
7	1	-	-	1	(0.18)
Total	162	331	36	529	
	(30.6)	(62.6)	(6.8)		(100.0)

say in other matters may not be correlated with exercising choice in matters of reproduction.

Another important reason for the lack of contraceptive use is the desire to have more sons, both among male and female respondents. The differential evaluation of male and female children in this matter is important for its implications for conscious efforts to limit family size. The differential evaluation is in turn both a function and a symptom of inherent gender bias.

As has been discussed earlier, poverty can restrict reproductive choice. Per capita income has been identified as the primary indicator of economic status. It is found that contraceptive use is positively correlated with rise in per capita income. There is a marked rise in contraceptive use among couples where per capita income is Rs 1,500 per annum or more. Poverty, by affecting chances for survival, access to health and nutrition, makes it imperative for couples to have large number of children. Thus, higher contraceptive use in economically well-off categories would imply that they have greater choice.

Landholding, as another indicator of economic status, is less significant in our sample. Most of the data consist of marginal land owners. Current contraceptive use is about 30 per cent in this sample, and there is some evidence of increase with increase in the size of land owned, though only 10 per cent own more than 5 acres. The percentage of couples using contraceptives increases (by 7 per cent or more) in the categories that own semi-*pucca* and *pucca* houses rather than *kutcha* ones. The greater incidence of contraceptive use in people owning a fairly large piece of land or *pucca* houses suggests that these economic assets provide security, alleviate poverty and increase the choice available to couples.

TABLE 9A. ANNUAL HOUSEHOLD INCOME BY CONTRACEPTIVE USE AS ANSWERED BY FEMALE RESPONDENTS

Annual Household Income (Rs)	Current Contraceptive Use			Total	(%)
	Using	Not Using	No Response/ Do not Know		
<2,500	6	15	2	23	(4.3)
2,500 - 5,000	19	48	2	69	(13.0)
5,000 - 7,500	14	71	6	91	(17.2)
7,500 - 10,000	20	43	7	70	(13.2)
10,000 - 15,000	43	62	7	112	(21.2)
15,000 - 20,000	20	35	2	57	(10.8)
20,000 - 30,000	19	32	6	57	(10.8)
30,000 - 40,000	6	10	3	19	(3.6)
40,000 - 50,000	5	6	-	11	(2.1)
>50,000	10	9	1	20	(3.8)
Total	162 (30.6)	331 (62.6)	36 (6.8)	529	(100.0)

TABLE 9B. ANNUAL HOUSEHOLD INCOME BY CONTRACEPTIVE USE AS ANSWERED BY MALE RESPONDENTS

Annual Household Income (Rs)	Current Contraceptive Use			Total	(%)
	Using	Not Using	No Response/ Do not Know		
<2,500	8	14	1	23	(4.3)
2,500 - 5,000	20	42	7	69	(13.0)
5,000 - 7,500	13	70	8	91	(17.2)
7,500 - 10,000	23	43	4	70	(13.2)
10,000 - 15,000	42	57	13	112	(21.2)
15,000 - 20,000	24	25	8	57	(10.8)
20,000 - 30,000	25	25	7	57	(10.8)
30,000 - 40,000	4	11	4	19	(3.6)
40,000 - 50,000	5	4	2	11	(3.1)
>50,000	11	8	1	20	(3.8)
Total	175 (33.1)	299 (56.5)	55 (10.4)	529	(100.0)

Poverty is also considered to affect reproductive choice because it is correlated with a high incidence of child mortality. In our sample, too, in families where one or more children have died, contraceptive use is much lower than in families where none have died. As poverty in these cases via child mortality provides a natural check on family size, the couples probably are not willing to use contraceptives.

Apart from poverty and gender inequality, there would be other factors that may spur the realization and need for active participation in limiting family size. However, in the sample, while 66 per cent couples discuss contraception sometimes, not even 10 per cent discuss it frequently. Whereas discussing sometimes is not correlated with actual use, frequent discussions do lead to much greater contraceptive use. Families where contraceptive use is discussed frequently may be characterized by better status and greater decision-making authority of women. The husband-wife relationship could also be such that more democratic decision-making is possible in such families as compared to those where contraceptive use is discussed rarely.

Differences in Male and Female Perceptions

In 529 out of the 1,078 households surveyed, women in the 15-49 years age group as well as their husbands were questioned on a number of issues. A comparison of the answers that were given by the women and the corresponding responses of their husbands present an interesting picture of differences in perceptions and awareness.

A large majority of women expect to depend on their sons in old age. More men say that depending on daughters is a possibility. Again on questions of educating daughters *vis-à-vis* sons, more women than men seem to subscribe to greater gender bias: a larger percentage of women have higher ambition for their sons' education than their daughters'. In comparison, men harbour a greater degree of egalitarian ambition for their sons and daughters.

This kind of gender equality does not, however, extend to men's perception about their wives. In response to just about every question asked of men and their wives to elicit information on the degree of autonomy women enjoy with respect to various matters, more men have persistently come out with statements that deny such autonomy to women. Many more men than their wives, for instance, consider that women do not and should not decide whether or not they should work outside the home, or have a say in matters dealing with children's education, or similar issues. In other words, the data seem to suggest that women think that they have a greater degree of autonomy in many things than their husbands are prepared to admit. Nevertheless, when it comes to their children, be it old age support or children's education, women appear to have imbibed traditional gender discriminatory values in a greater degree than their husbands. This is an interesting hypothesis which needs further investigation.

Some of the most interesting contrasts in male and female responses come up in the area of contraceptive use. Out of a total of 529 cases surveyed, in 103 cases, i.e. nearly 20 per cent, there is a contradiction in male and female reporting on current contraceptive use. The percentage is higher if we club the 'no response' cases with those that have reported 'no use' among both males and females. When asked whether they intend to use any contraceptive method in the next twelve months, the discrepancy is even higher.

The picture is even more revealing when contraceptive use is classified by type of use. Male reporting of use of male contraceptive is far higher than the corresponding reporting by females. For instance, as against 36 husbands who say that they currently use the condom, only 11 wives have corroborated the claim. Even male sterilization claims made by the husbands outstrip the reporting by their wives. When questioned about intention of contraceptive use in the next twelve months by contraceptive type, the imbalance within the family on responsibility for contraception is even more clearly brought out.

One thing men and women seem to agree on: many more couples intend to depend on female contraception methods. Only one couple agreed on male sterilization or vasectomy as compared to 29 on tubectomy. Four women intend to go in for the latter without their husbands' knowledge, while the large majority of couples were undecided.

Multivariate Analysis: Some Results

The survey questionnaire used for generating the data under review is very large. In all, each questionnaire generates values for nearly 1,500 variables spread over a number of modules. Our major concern in this paper has been to sift through this large body of data in order to understand the nature of linkages between reproductive behaviour on the one hand and gender inequality and poverty on the other. This section reports the results of some preliminary investigations we have carried out in this direction using multiple regression techniques (refer Table 10).

Ideally, issues such as those of fertility, child mortality, reproductive health and reproductive choice should be analysed within a simultaneous-

TABLE 10. MULTIVARIATE EQUATIONS

	\multicolumn{6}{c}{Dependent Variables}
	Total Pregnancies			Total Live Births		
Variables	Equation 1	Equation 2	Equation 3	Equation 1	Equation 2	Equation 3
Constant	-2.129	-2.111	-1.680	-2.108	-2.128	-1.753
	(-4.21)	(-4.21)	(-3.13)	(-4.66)	(-4.74)	(-3.65)
FA13	0.216	0.217	0.218	0.211	0.211	0.212
	(21.75)	(21.83)	(22.10)	(23.65)	(23.71)	(24.00)
FF3A1	-0.011	-	-	-8.410E-04	-	-
	(-1.10)	-	-	(0.90)	-	-
FF3B1	-	-0.013	-0.015	-	-7.800E-03	-8.610E-03
	-	(-1.27)	(-1.43)	-	(-0.84)	(-0.92)
FD3	-	-	-0.88	-	-	-0.96
	-	-	(-0.76)	-	-	(-0.92)
D3	-	-	-2.878E-03	-	-	-0.066
	-	-	(-0.03)	-	-	(-0.72)
PC	-2.232E-04	-2.246E-04	-2.369E-04	-2.481E-04	-2.493E-04	-2.538E-04
	(-4.29)	(-4.31)	(-4.50)	(-5.32)	(-5.35)	(-5.38)
PC2	5.184E-04	5.240E-09	5.930E-09	5.880E-09	5.921E-09	6.313E-09
	(1.86)	(1.88)	(2.12)	(2.36)	(2.37)	(2.51)
BIO	-0.079	-0.067	-0.139	-0.78	-0.070	-0.119
	(-0.45)	(-0.38)	(-0.82)	(-0.50)	(-0.45)	(-78)
B13	0.170	0.175	-	0.144	0.147	-
	(1.63)	(1.67)	-	(1.53)	(1.56)	-
B3AD1	-	-	-0.260	-	-	-0.97
	-	-	(-1.43)	-	-	(1.21)
B3AD2	-	-	0.026	-	-	-0.013
	-	-	(0.14)	-	-	(-0.08)
FD4	-0.107	-0.118	0.011	-0.112	-0.122	-0.033
	(-0.57)	(-0.63)	(0.04)	(-0.67)	(-0.73)	(0.13)
D4	0.39	0.040	-0.025	0.032	0.034	0.118
	(0.21)	(0.21)	(-0.08)	(0.20)	(0.21)	(0.44)
FD5A	-0.472	-0.465	-0.372	-0.373	-0.367	-0.318
	(-2.73)	(-2.68)	(-2.25)	(-2.40)	(-2.37)	(-2.15)
D5A	0.181	0.177	0.117	0.199	0.197	0.103
	(0.89)	(0.88)	(0.64)	(1.10)	(1.09)	(0.63)
FD5B	0.164	0.155	-	0.011	5.363E-03	-
	(0.83)	(0.78)	-	(0.06)	(0.03)	-
D5B	-0.212	-0.211	-	-0.299	-0.300	-
	(-1.07)	(-1.06)	-	(-1.69)	(-1.69)	-
FK5	0.522	0.520	-	0.416	0.417	-
	(0.99)	(0.98)	-	(0.88)	(0.88)	-

(Contd)

TABLE 10. *(Contd)*

	Dependent Variables					
	Total Pregnancies			Total Live Births		
Variables	Equation 1	Equation 2	Equation 3	Equation 1	Equation 2	Equation 3
FK4	0.073	0.092	-	0.024	(0.39)	-
	(0.40)	(0.50)	-	(0.15)	(0.24)	-
FK3	0.047	0.040	-	0.107	0.102	-
	(0.31)	(0.26)	-	(0.77)	(0.74)	-
HIGHEA	-	-	-9.57	-	-	-1.013
	-	-	(-1.56)	-	-	(-1.85)
MIDDLEEA	-	-	0.295	-	-	0.291
	-	-	(0.86)	-	-	(0.94)
NOEA	-	-	0.305	-	-	0.277
	-	-	(0.82)	-	-	(0.83)
HIGHPA	-	-	-0.043	-	-	0.126
	-	-	(0.26)	-	-	(0.86)
MIDDLEPA	-	-	-0.069	-	-	-0.097
	-	-	(-0.16)	-	-	(-0.24)
FJ5	0.078	0.082	0.103	0.046	0.048	0.057
	(0.95)	(0.96)	(0.04)	(0.62)	(0.65)	(0.77)
R^2	0.441	0.441	0.442	0.487	0.487	0.489
Adjusted R^2	0.429	0.430	0.428	0.477	0.477	0.476
F	37.525	37.571	31.672	45.236	45.222	38.146
Sample Size	793	793	793	793	793	793

LIST OF VARIABLES

FA13	Age of female respondents
FF3A1	Age at marriage for females
FF3B1	Age at *gauna* for females
FD3	Years of schooling completed for females
D3	Years of schooling completed for males
PC	Per capita household income
PC2	Per capita income squared
B10	Landholding
B13	Livestock ownership
B3AD1	House type—*kutcha*
B3AD2	House type—*semi-pucca*
FD4	Ability to read for females
D4	Ability to read for males
FD5A	Exposure to radio for females
D5A	Exposure to radio for males
FD5B	Exposure to TV for females
D5B	Exposure to TV for males
FK5	Any land in female respondent's name

FK4	Whether females earn independently
FK3	Whether permission from elders for females to purchase items for personal use
High EA	High economic autonomy implies
	(a) The female gets cash in hand for household expenditure; (b) She can buy items of personal use without elder's permission; (c) She has full control over her own income.
Middle EA	Middle economic autonomy implies
	(a) She gets cash in hand for household expenditure; (b) She can buy items of personal use without elder's permission; (c) She gives part of her own income to her husband but she has control over the rest of it.
No EA	No economic autonomy is constructed from:
	(a) She does not get any cash in hand for household expenditure; (b) She has to seek elders' permission to buy items of personal use; (c) She does not earn independently or gives all her income to her husband and other members of the household.
High PA	High personal autonomy is constructed from:
	(a) The respondent has a say in going out to work, education of children and care during children's illness; (b) She goes outside the village without permission from her husband or elders and alone.
Middle PA	Middle personal autonomy implies
	(a) The respondent has a say in going out to work, and is allowed to go outside the village without permission and alone but does not have a say in children's education or care of their illness. OR (b) She has a say in her children's education and care during their illness but has no say in going out to work and cannot to outside the village without permission and alone.
FJ5	Current contraceptive use among couples.

equations framework. The survey unfortunately has very little information on reproductive health. Also, although there are long sections on pregnancy history, it is difficult to link this information to the phasing of contraceptive use, if any. We resisted using a simultaneous-equation framework and have experimented with single-equation estimation of structural equations at the cost of some efficiency and bias of the estimators.

The dependent variable in these equations is fertility behaviour as represented by the number of pregnancies or the number of live births among women in reproductive age brackets. Ideally, these could have been adjusted for the difference in remaining reproductive spans of women in different age groups to net out the effect of age.[5] One method of doing this would be to use the estimated distribution of children expected to be born to women in different age groups in Uttar Pradesh from the Sample Registration System (SRS) data to arrive at fertility indices normalized by age.[5] We have chosen instead to use the number of pregnancies as reported in the data and have used age of the respondent as one of the explanatory variables. Predictably, this comes out with very significant t-values in all the equations. Given the current age of the respondent, the lower the age at marriage (FF3A1), or better, the lower the age at *gauna* (FF3B1), the higher is the reproductive span lived through by a respondent at the time of the survey, and therefore, the higher will be the number of pregnancies, other things remaining constant. Both these variables come out with positive and significant t-values in our equations.

Given the large size of the questionnaire, the set of variables from which we could choose our other explanatory variables was uncomfortably large. The task was made easier by the fact that a number of these variables are of peripheral relevance to the central concern of this paper, which is to unravel the linkages between poverty, gender and fertility behaviour. Use of some others for running regressions was ruled out since some sections in the questionnaire—as for instance, the module on detailed labour use pattern by members of the household—have been left blank by many. We had problems in choosing indicators of the respondent's autonomy within the household as a factor which could influence reproductive choice. The number of questions asked to elicit the extent of control the woman has in her day-to-day living situation were many. We clubbed them in groups, and developed indices of the woman's economic and personal autonomy to be used as qualitative explanatory variables. Alternative indicators were used to measure the level of the respondent's awareness, the economic status of the household, personal characteristics of the husband, perceptions about reproduction and contraception by husband and wife and indicators of communication within the marital relationship.

A SUMMARY OF FINDINGS

An interesting result that has repeatedly surfaced with this data set, which perhaps runs counter to the received wisdom in this area in recent years, is that female literacy as represented by years of schooling, or levels of school achievement, has come up with totally insignificant t-values in most equations we ran, while another variable, which we tried as a surrogate for awareness, i.e. female exposure to radio broadcast (FD5A1) appears with much greater explanatory power. The result is interesting because it suggests that the goodness or otherwise of an indicator in terms of capturing the essence of an unquantified and unquantifiable qualitative variable such as awareness, may vary significantly depending on the context within which it is embedded (cf. the introductory section above). Another significant finding in the fertility equations is the powerful impact of per capita income as explanatory variable for fertility as opposed, once again, to received wisdom in this respect. Since one of our central concerns had been to delineate the links between poverty and reproduction, we chose a number of indicators for both variables. Among the indicators we chose for poverty were per capita income (PCI), size of landholding, house type and asset/livestock ownership, of which, the best results were obtained with respect to per capita income.

While the linear specification did not produce good results, t-values were very significant when we introduced a quadratic term. Thus, fertility appears to be strongly correlated to per capita income in a parabolic manner, with high fertility associated with very low and very high levels of per capita income and dropping in between. The lowest predicted fertility levels are reached typically at levels of per capita incomes that are significantly higher than the sample average.

We experimented with a range of female autonomy variables thrown up by the survey. Most were of a qualitative or categorical nature. Some of these have been reported in the equations. By and large, they have come out with a not-too-significant explanatory power. An attempt was made to construct some indices of different dimensions of female autonomy. Apart from the 'high economic autonomy' index, no other case turned out to have significant explanatory power.

CONCLUDING REMARKS

A number of studies in recent times have explored the determinants of fertility behaviour and contraceptive use among women. Our attempt in this paper has been to shed fresh light on these categories with the help of data from a household survey carried out in five districts of Uttar Pradesh under a project designed to bring out the links between poverty, gender inequality and reproductive choice.

The elaborate multi-dimensional reach of the questionnaire has made it possible to explore the complex interlinkages of many factors that affect women's reproductive behaviour. Our investigations reveal that poverty as measured by per capita household incomes is a strong determinant of fertility behaviour, albeit in a non-linear fashion. Media exposure, especially exposure to radio broadcasts, is another factor that comes out as significantly and positively linked with use of contraceptives. Child mortality, predictably, has a deterrent effect on contraceptive use, while higher literacy levels are linked with higher incidence of use.

The data generated by the Uttar Pradesh survey clearly reveal that even for one-third of the women in the reproductive age group who have reported contraceptive use, such use can be barely said to reflect evidence of exercising reproductive choice. For a large majority of these women, contraceptive choice is limited to tubectomy, and most of them reveal, on questioning, their unhappiness with the terminal nature of the method, apart from post-terminal health problems. Thus, even though contraceptive technology has reached the far corners of rural India in a big way, the nature of choice for poor women is highly constrained.

NOTES

1. The paper is based on a micro-study that forms part of a larger project titled 'Poverty, Gender Inequality and Reproductive Choice'. The project is funded by the MacArthur Foundation. The schedules were fielded in several villages in Uttar Pradesh and Karnataka by the National Council of Applied Economic Research (NCAER). The data analysed here pertain only to the Uttar Pradesh sample.
2. See for instance, Murthi, Guio and Dreze (1995), *Mortality, Fertility and Gender Bias in India: A District Level Analysis*. DEP No. 61, June, London School of Economics, London.
3. See Dreze and Sen (1995), *India: Economic Development and Social Opportunity*, Oxford University Press, Oxford.
4. See for details, N.H. Antia and K. Bhatia (eds.), 1993, *People's Health in People's Hands*, FRCH, Bombay.
5. See for instance, statement 21 titled 'Percent Cumulative Fertility by Age, India and major states', 1993, p. 44 of *Fertility and Mortality Indicators*, 1993, Sample Registration System, Registrar General of India, New Delhi.

REFERENCES

Altekar, A.S., 1959. *The Position of Women in Hindu Civilization*, Motilal Banarsidass, Delhi.
Antia, N.H. and K. Bhatia (eds.), 1993. *People's Health in People's Hands: A Model for Panchayati Raj*, FRCH, Bombay.
Basu, Alaka M., 1992. *Culture, the Status of Women and Demographic Behaviour*, Clarendon Press, Oxford.
Berger, Marge, 1994. 'The Meaning of Motherhood, Fatherhood and Fertility: For women who do and women who don't have children', *Reproductive Health Matters*, London.
Bruce, J. and Dwyer (eds.), 1988. Introduction, in *A Home Divided: Women and Income in the Third World*, Stanford University Press, California.
Cleland, J. and Rodriguez, 1988. 'The Effect of Parental Education on Marital Fertility in Developing Countries', *Population Studies*, 42(3,4).

Cochrane, S.H., 1979. *Fertility and Education: What do We Really Know?* Johns Hopkins University Press, Baltimore.
————, 1982. 'Parental Education and Child Health: Intracountry Evidence', *Health Policy and Education* 2(3,4).
Dasgupta, M. et al., 1995. *Women's Health in India: Risk and Vulnerability*, Oxford University Press, Bombay.
Desai, Sonalde, 1994. *Gender Inequalities and Demographic Behaviour: India*, Report by the Population Council, USA.
Dixon, Muller, 1978. *Rural Women at Work: Strategies for Development in South Asia*, Johns Hopkins University Press, Baltimore.
————, 1993. *Population Policies and Women's Rights*, Praeger, London.
Dixon, Ruth, 1975. 'Women's Rights and Fertility', Report on Population, *Family Planning*, No. 17.
Duggal, Ravi et al., 1995. 'Health Expenditure across States: Parts I and II', *Economic and Political Weekly* 30(15, 16).
Germain, Adrienne, 1975. 'Status and Roles of Women as Factors in Fertility Behaviour: A Policy Analysis', *Studies in Family Planning*, 6 July.
————, et al., 1994. 'Setting a New Agenda: Sexual and Reproductive Health and Rights', in Gita Sen et al. (eds.), *Population Policies Reconsidered: Health, Empowerment and Rights*, Harvard Centre for Population and Development Studies, Massachusetts and IWHC, New York.
Goode, William J., 1961. 'Family Disorganization', in R.K. Merton and R.A. Nisket (eds.), *Contemporary Social Problems*, Harcourt, Brace and World, New York.
Graham, Hillary, 1993. *Hardship and Health in Women's Lives*, Harvester Wheatsheaf.
Guilleband, John, 1991. *The Pill*, Oxford University Press, Oxford.
Institute of Social Studies Trust, 1996. *Poverty, Gender Inequality and Reproductive Choice*. 3 volumes.
Jeffery, Patrick, et al., 1989. *Labour Pains and Labour Power: Women and Childbearing in India*, Zed Books, London.
Kabir, Sandra, 1989. 'Causes and Consequences of Unwanted Pregnancy from Asian Women's Perspective', *International Journal of Gynaecology Obstetrics Supplement* 3.
Kalpana, Ram, 1994. 'Medical Management and Giving Birth: Responses of Coastal Women in Tamil Nadu', *Reproductive Health Matters* 4.
Karkal, Mohini et al., 1995. 'Women, Health and Development', *Radical Journal of Health* 1 (Bombay).
Karve, Irawati, 1965. *Kinship Organisation in India*, Asia Publishing House, Bombay.
Krishnaji, N., 1987. 'Poverty and Sex Ratio: Some Data and Speculations', *Economic and Political Weekly* 22.
Mahmud, S., 1993. 'Female Power: A Key Variable in Understanding the Relationship Between Women's Work and Fertility', Bangladesh Institute of Development Studies (unpublished manuscript).
———— and A.M. Johnston, 1994. 'Women's Status, Empowerment and Reproductive Outcomes', in Gita Sen et al. (eds.), *Population Policies Reconsidered: Health Empowerment and Rights*, Harvard Centre for Population and Development Studies, Massachusetts and IWHC, New York.
Miller, Barbara, 1981. *The Endangered Sex*, Cornell University Press, Ithaca.
————, 1993. 'On Poverty, Child Survival and Gender: Models and Misperception', *Third World Planning Review* 15.

Mink, Stephen, 1992. *Poverty, Population and the Environment*, Development Report, World Bank.

Murthi, Mamta et al., 1995. *Mortality, Fertility and Gender Bias in India: A District Level Analysis*, Development Economics Research Programme, DEP, June, No. 61, London School of Economics, London.

Nelson, N., 1979. *Why Has Development Neglected Rural Women: A Review of South Asian Literature*, Pergamon Press, Oxford.

Ravindran, Sundari T.K., 1993. 'Users' Perspectives on Fertility Regulation Methods', *Economic and Political Weekly* 28(46, 47).

Richardson, Diane, 1992. *Women, Motherhood and Childbearing*, Macmillan, London.

Roberts, Helen, 1992. *Women's Health Matters*, Routledge, London.

Safilios-Rothschild, C., 1982. 'Female Power, Autonomy and Demographic Change in the Third World', in R. Anker et al. (eds.), *Women's Roles and Population Trends in the Third World*, Croom Helm, London.

United Nations, 1987. *Fertility Behaviour in the Context of Development: Evidence from the World Fertility Survey*, Department of International Economics and Social Affairs, New York.

Williams, P.J., 1991. *The Alchemy of Race and Rights*, Harvard University Press, Cambridge.

World Bank, 1991. *Gender and Poverty in India: A World Bank Country Study*, World Bank, Washington D.C.

————, 1992. *Poverty Reduction Handbook and Operational Derivative*.

Youssef, N.H., 1982. 'The Inter-relation Between the Division of Labour in the Household, Women's Roles and their Impact on Fertility', in R. Anker et al. (eds.), *Women's Roles and Population Trends in the Third World*, Croom Helm, London.

The Contours of Reproductive Choice for Poor Women: Findings from a Micro Survey

SWAPNA MUKHOPADHYAY
SUREKHA GARIMELLA

INTRODUCTION

Reproductive choice and reproductive rights are two of the current buzzwords in feminist discourse. From 'population and development' related issues to human rights concerns or concerns about reproductive technologies, liberated and informed debate has been resounding with references to these words. There is a concern about the reproductive rights of poor rural women of developing countries, their rights on their bodies and the need to remove constraints on their reproductive choices. In this paper we have made a modest attempt to chart out some parameters of such choice, with the help of a small but intensive survey conducted under an ISST project completed in 1995.[1]

The parameters of choice that we intend to explore in this paper have emerged out of a process of trying to define the constituent elements of a woman-friendly population policy. The focus of our interest is the notion of 'unwanted pregnancy' as women perceive it, and the way they deal with it. Women's perception of choice, their ability to exercise choice and the material conditions that influence these choices are considered. Before it can become a choice between contraception alternatives, the question is primarily one of women's self-esteem and autonomy.

A survey was conducted in four locations in the country to chalk out the parameters of such choice. Information sought was centred around negotiation of sexual relations and sexual subordination within the marital relationship. The material conditions that influence reproductive choice were addressed by looking into the supply and the demand aspects of the issue—the availability of necessary facilities representing the supply dimensions, as well as variables such as perceptions on contraception and per capita expenditure as surrogate for effective demand. The incidence and reporting of abortion, use of contraception, perception of pregnancies and reproductive health problems—all these go to define the nature of choice. Our attempt has been to ask questions on relatively unexplored areas, to plug the hazy areas in existing knowledge base, rather than to field a comprehensive questionnaire encompassing all aspects of reproductive choice.

THE BACKDROP

Reproductive choice, which has generally been taken to be synonymous with fertility regulation, has been the subject of a fair amount of research in the past decade. Information generated pertains mainly to conditions that could possibly affect the reproductive choices that women and households make. Largely the understanding of choice has been centred around the number of children a woman would want to have and her need for and access to contraceptive devices.

Factors likely to affect reproductive choice are infant and child mortality, desire for children—in particular male children, women's participation in the labour market, their educational status, availability of health and family welfare services and socio-economic status of the household. The focus here is on the effect of gender inequality on reproductive behaviour. Inequality has been expressed mainly in terms of the extent to which women have autonomy within a marital relationship and within the family (Dyson & Moore 1983) and in terms of prestige, power and control over social and economic resources (Mason 1984). Family and kinship indicators defining autonomy include seclusion and marriage patterns, nature of the household, dowry, inheritance patterns, etc. Women's educational status, their participation in economic production, control over wages, etc., are some of the other indicators (Jeejeebhoy 1991).

Factors influencing fertility are also thought to be strongly influenced by gender relations within and beyond the household. Women and men often have conflicting interests and men tend to reap the benefits of large families while women bear the costs (Kabeer 1992).

Generally, women's improved educational status is thought to be associated with better bargaining power, with a resultant increase in control over resources. Within the home it is thought to improve their knowledge and skills required for increasing their decision-making power, build up resistance to traditional norms and help in developing a more equal relationship with the spouse (Jeejeebhoy 1991). Women's participation in economic activities may not by itself necessarily be an indicator of their autonomy. The relative autonomy of poor working or earning women may not also exceed that of non-earning women of higher economic status. Woman's control over her income and not merely work status may therefore have an important bearing on autonomy (Jeejeebhoy 1991).

Family and kinship structures that are believed to affect woman's status are the practice of exogamy, severance of links with her natal home after marriage and inability to contribute economically to her natal family. Of interest are also indicators of status and their effect on fertility. Status to some extent can be assessed by the number of children a couple will have in the absence of fertility regulation, women's status as it affects the demand for children, mainly male children, and finally women's status as it affects knowledge, attitudes and practice of fertility regulation.

Age at marriage also can be an important determinant of low degree of reproductive control resulting in higher fertility. Low female status results in early age at marriage, and consequent inability to regulate fertility.

Another good reflector of women's low status and gender inequality is the number of desired children, mainly male. Perceived value of children, male or female, greatly influences the desire for children. There is evidence that son preference and family size are negatively related to women's status (Cain 1984). Woman's lack of power itself forms the basis of demand for children, and sons in particular, to legitimize her own status and ensure economic survival (Jeejeebhoy 1991).

Against this larger backdrop, the links between the desire to regulate fertility and actual contraceptive use may yet be tenuous. Factors normally attributed to poor contraceptive use are family planning measures, lack of availability of women-friendly services, and negative household and spouse attitudes towards family planning. Unequal power relationships within the household curtail female autonomy and impinge on the exercise of choice. The survey was designed to capture some of these less articulated parameters of choice.

THE ISSUES

The issues sought to be explored in the survey were: (a) some dimensions of reproductive choice; (b) unwanted pregnancy; (c) abortion; (d) sexual negotiation within the family; (e) family planning; (f) men's perceptions; and (g) infertility.

Reproductive choice: some dimensions. Some of the questions we addressed pertain to women's control over their own bodies within the context of their social situation. This is different from the thrust of the debate on 'reproductive choice' which confines itself solely, or mainly to the nature of choice between alternative contraceptives. Issues sought to be explored were of the following kind:

— Does the question/notion of choice at all exist in the harsh reality of a poor woman's life?
— If choice exists, what is its nature in deciding the number and timing of children?
— To what extent is she able to negotiate sexual relations with her partner?

Unwanted pregnancy. Related to choice is the question of 'unwanted pregnancy'. FHS (Family Health Survey) studies in the early 1960s found evidence that a large percentage of currently pregnant women did not want to be pregnant in the first place. We sought to unravel the incidence and nature of such 'unwanted pregnancies' by trying to explore questions like:

— Does the notion of an 'unwanted pregnancy' really exist in a culture where rearing of children is viewed as the primary purpose of a woman's life?
— If women do express that a certain pregnancy is unwanted, what are the reasons attributed to this feeling?
— What do women do in case an 'unwanted pregnancy' does occur? Do they take some conscious action about it?
— Who and what conditions influence their decisions about an 'unwanted pregnancy'?

Abortion. Abortion relates directly to the earlier set of questions. What are women's feelings on abortion? How do they place themselves in relation to other women in the community regarding this issue? How deeply do they reflect the prevalent notions of rightness and wrongness of having 'induced abortion'? The questions posed were:

— What are the options available to women if they opt for an abortion? How aware are they of existing methods and facilities?
— What conditions and people influence decisions on whether or not to have an abortion?

— What is the extent of awareness on existing legal provisions on abortion?

Sexual negotiation within the family. Within the existing patriarchal family system, a woman's voice often goes unheard, while there are social sanctions against a woman who is perceived to undermine her duty towards her partner and his family. By the time a girl is married she has by and large internalized recognized norms of behaviour that are expected of her. As a direct offshoot of this, we were interested in understanding how women negotiate space for themselves, if any, in the relationship with their partners/families. Hence, there was an effort to probe the existing notions of women's duties towards their partners especially in the domain of sexual relations. We tried to explore the following issues:

— How prevalent is the incidence of 'forced sex' within marriage?
— How does the family react in case she refuses to have sex with her partner?
— Can she depend upon the family for some support if she makes such a decision?
— Does her partner abide by the prevalent religious norms regarding sexual contact on religious and other occasions?
— Is there any cognizable link between perceived sexual oppression and 'unwanted pregnancies' and the manner in which women articulate this?

Family planning. We investigated family planning practices or their absence in the context of women's life situations, their health status in general and reproductive health in particular. Some of the questions addressed were:

— What is the level of awareness of methods and perceptions of usefulness *vis-à-vis* actual use of contraceptive methods?
— What are the most commonly used measures of family planning? Which of the partners uses any chosen method and why?
— Do women experience health complications on use of contraception and, if so, what remedial action do they take?

Men's perceptions. We tried to probe men's perceptions on a number of issues. Responses were sought regarding their own and their spouses' duties towards each other and what their reactions would be if they felt that the wife failed to do her duties. This was considered important in bringing out the contradictions between men's and women's perceptions, as impinging on the objective reality. Among other things, men were questioned on:

— The extent to which they were informed about their family's health problems, especially those of their wives.
— Use of contraceptives and their perceptions on contraceptive use—induced health problems for their wives and for themselves.
— Their views on abortion and how they would react in case the wife expressed a desire to have one.

Infertility. Reproductive choice has largely been discussed in the context of women wanting to curtail pregnancies. But what about choice for women who want to have children but are not able to conceive? To answer this question information on the experiences of infertile women, related to the pressures of society and family that they face was also elicited.

PROJECT DESIGN AND SAMPLE SURVEY

DESIGNING A 'WOMAN-FRIENDLY POPULATION POLICY': AN ISST/UNFPA PROJECT

As stated earlier, issues to be discussed emerged as a part of the process of defining the elements of a 'woman-friendly population policy'. This project was undertaken by ISST between June 1993 and March 1995. It was structured into two phases. Phase I involved a series of consultations with rural women with the help of seven voluntary organizations who were familiar with the local poor women and broadly represented the north, south, east and west of the country. The findings of Phase I were broadly as follows:

— Non-functional, inaccessible health services and unhappiness with the government family planning programme were cited as major problems the women faced. The necessity for decent functional health services, access to correct health information and health education was also expressed.

— Dissatisfaction was expressed with unemployment, poverty, lack of water facilities, sanitation and other basic infrastructural facilities. These issues largely overshadowed the question of fertility regulation (cf. ISST 1994).

To a large extent these reflect the current concerns being debated in the population and development debate. To arrive at a family planning strategy which is women-sensitive and women-friendly, therefore, one needs to probe deeper into the lives, beliefs and perceptions of poor women burdened down by economic and social pressures which have perhaps been internalized in such a fashion that they are not perceived as pressures at all.

Phase I was characterized by individual and group discussions centred around issues like health needs, reproductive rights, contraception, etc., which were held on the basis of open-ended checklists prepared by the various groups. Questions related to reproductive choice—perceptions of choice, ability to exercise choice and the material conditions to influence this ability—were not discussed in great detail.

Phase II sought to address these issues in greater depth. The information in this phase was collected on various dimensions of reproductive choice through a structured questionnaire and focus group discussions.

The idea was to gain an understanding on 'reproductive choice' as perceived by women and incorporate these perceptions and needs in the woman-friendly family planning strategy. The survey was conducted for 200 women in the reproductive age group in each of the four locations.[2] In 50 of the households, Section VII of the questionnaire designed for men was fielded to an adult male of the household. The present paper is based on information from one urban location (Delhi), and one rural location (the Kumaon hills of Uttar Pradesh). The cleaned and edited data set contains 159 schedules from the Delhi sample and 183 schedules from Kumaon.

The Delhi sample. The survey was conducted in the Ambedkar Nagar *basti* of Rama Krishna Puram, New Delhi. The notion of family for most *basti* dwellers is a group of people related to each other by blood, through the male descendants. The resident population in the *basti* are encroachers, predominantly belonging to scheduled castes. Brahmins and Thakurs are present in negligible numbers. Muslims constitute a very small proportion.

Women are mainly illiterate and so are most of the men. Amongst the literates, the minimum level of education is up to the primary level, while the maximum level of education is secondary; not even 1 per cent of the literates have higher secondary education. Children in most families go to school, though the parents complain about their lack of interest in studies, especially classes beyond the fifth.

The scheduled castes generally work as *safai karamcharis* (sweepers). In the two *Sulabh Sauchalayas* constructed in the area for public convenience, the *karamcharis* are outsiders who stay within the compound of *Sulabh Sauchalaya*. Both men and women work as *safai karamcharis* employed by the government, with women employees in negligible numbers. Roughly 25 per cent of the women go out for work, most of the rest working in residential complexes as sweepers. About 20-30 per cent of the working population (both men and women) are daily wagers. In the working population 5 per cent of the men are vendors, selling fruits, vegetables, sweets, eggs and *pakoras* on the roadside. Muslim men, and women from the forward castes do not go out for work.

People in general seem content with whatever basic services they have, exceptions being water, electricity and toilet facilities. Even here, they are not dissatisfied as such, though they do have problems such as lack of water sources, which leads to large queues often ending in fights. People find the water clean, safe and hygienic, and therefore drink it straight. Many do not use the chlorine tablets supplied free for cleaning the water, and even those who do, do so as long as they get the tablets.

The women have a major problem on account of lack of proper toilet facilities. The *Sulabh Sauchalayas* are poorly maintained, a statement confirmed by first-hand experience. Most women therefore make use of a nearby park, also referred to as jungle or *nallah*, and thus become vulnerable to the increasing crimes against women.

There is no PHC in the *basti*. There is a dispensary run by an NGO by the name of Asia Clinic/Dispensary.

Television sets, music systems, room coolers and table fans are commonly found, and so are ceiling fans in houses with *pucca* roofs. Bicycles are commonly used by men to go out to work.

Very few scheduled caste households have agricultural land in the villages. The land owned by others is a few *bighas* only in size, generally tilled with agricultural labourers using non-mechanized implements. A couple of scheduled caste families are into piggery and also sell pork.

Roughly 8 per cent of the families fall in the monthly expenditure bracket of Rs 500 and below; 30 per cent in Rs 1,000-2,000; 55 per cent in Rs 2,000-3,000; 7 per cent in Rs 3,000-5,000.

The Kumaon sample. The hilly region in northern Uttar Pradesh is called Kumaon, and comprises three districts, namely Almora, Nainital and Pithoragarh. The southern part of Kumaon, popularly known as *terai* is flat.

There are both joint and nuclear families, primarily Hindu, belonging to the scheduled castes and forward castes. Women in the sample have mostly studied up to the primary level (class V) and are unpaid family workers. Literacy levels of men are fairly high with many of them having graduated. Everyone has land and a house as this is a necessity to survive in the cold climate.

In Almora district, only the government hospital provides health services primarily. There are many non-governmental organizations but health-related areas are not their primary concern. A few organizations keep homeopathic medicines for minor ailments.

Gramin Uthan Samiti of Kapkot and Lakshmi Ashram of Kasauni are organizations working for women's development. Lakshmi Ashram has a dispensary dispensing homeopathic and ayurvedic medicines for general treatment. But people are neither given medicines nor any information on ailments or problems related to childbirth. Another organization, 'Sahabhagi Gramin Vikas' also works on health-related issues by organizing awareness camps, workshops, etc.

The health care services in the region comprise one government hospital at district headquarters, a PHC and MHC at block level, and 40 to 50 dispensaries in each block.

The regional health centres located 15 to 20 km from the average village in the hills are mostly inaccessible to patients. Those within reach are bereft of basic infrastructure and manpower.

SOME DESCRIPTIVE STATISTICS FROM THE SURVEY

Pregnancy profile of women. Information related to number of pregnancies and their outcomes gives the pregnancy profile presented in Table 1.

The average age at marriage for women in both Delhi and Kumaon ranged between 14 and 19 years. The average number of pregnancies was respectively around 3.92 and 3.14. About 30 per cent of the women from Delhi had some sort of ante-natal care; the rest did not have any care at all, and did not feel its necessity. In Kumaon only 22 per cent had some sort of ante-natal care. Reporting of health complications during pregnancy was minimal, but there were some references to extreme tiredness/weakness. In both groups, the majority of the women had their deliveries in their marital homes conducted mainly by untrained/local *dais*. Government facilities were also availed in some cases, more so in the Delhi sample. The Kumaon sample shows a very high proportion of miscarriages, reflecting the physical strain of living in hilly terrain as also the relative inaccessibility of medical facilities in the hills.

Women's reproductive health profile. Information regarding reproductive health status was generated on the basis of women's perception of illness, hence the indicators were a combination of symptoms and generalized problems. They are not strictly clinical categories.

The Kumaoni women were more vocal in expressing their problems than the Delhi sample. In both samples, women reported normally a combination of symptoms. A sizeable proportion of women reported white discharge and menstrual problems. A combination of giddiness, tiredness and breathlessness were all too common in both samples (Table 2).

A sizeable proportion of women from the Delhi sample did seek medical help but expressed unhappiness at the treatment received, on the ground that they were not cured and the problems kept recurring. A much lower proportion of Kumaoni women sought medical help, may be because of general paucity of medical services in the region. In both samples most of the women approached private facilities (Table 3).

Infertility. Common to the cases of infertility we came across are two factors: (a) the women carry the burden of infertility alone; and (b) they have a nagging fear of desertion by their husbands.

Women's views on contraception. This section seeks to give an overview of issues relating to awareness of contraceptive methods, notions of their usefulness, extent of use, who makes the decision regarding use or non-use and complications experienced by women on use.

Awareness of various methods of contraception was extensive in the urban samples, especially that from Delhi. The Kumaoni women exhibited lower level of awareness, but a higher degree of interest in knowing about available options. High levels of awareness in the Delhi sample could be due to the greater access to the visual and audio media (largely television and radio).

Uniformly in both samples, the women felt that contraception was useful, but this was not reflected in the actual use of methods of family planning. In fact, in all the samples more than two-thirds of the women

TABLE 1. PREGNANCY PROFILE

Profile	Delhi		Kumaon	
Total no. of women	159		183	
Total no. of pregnancies	623		575	
Average no. of pregnancies per woman	3.92		3.14	
Outcome of pregnancies:				
Live births	534	(85.7)	490	(85.2)
Still births	10	(1.6)	7	(1.2)
Miscarriages	36	(5.8)	54	(9.4)
Induced abortions	7	(1.1)	9	(1.6)
Currently pregnant	21	(3.4)	4	(0.7)
No details	15	(2.4)	11	(1.9)
Total	623	(100.0)	575	(100.0)

Note: Figures within brackets are percentages.

did not use any method at all. Among those who did, tubectomy was the most common and it was done on completion of the preferred family size. Among those who used IUD (mainly Copper-T) discontinuation was quite high on account of excessive bleeding.

The main reasons why women thought that contraception is useful are: (a) it is necessary to limit family size; (b) useful for spacing childbirths; (c) the belief that too many pregnancies can cause health problems for the women.

Family planning measures were adopted mainly based on mutual consent by the couple; in the sample from Delhi, however, a majority of women users had decided on their own to use whatever method they had adopted.

Preference for tubectomy could be attributed to the following reasons: (a) health complications with other methods and lack of proper information on the side-effects; (b) permanent nature of the operation; (c) opted mainly on completion of the preferred family size, the woman's decision to undergo tubectomy gets support from the family.

Reported incidence of complications due to contraceptive use is fairly high. This picture was uniform in all the four locations. The reported complications are mainly (a) persistent abdominal pain; (b) persistent back pain; (c) excessive bleeding; and (d) weakness.

For complications resulting from contraceptive use in the urban samples, a large proportion of women did seek medical treatment, but not in the rural areas, reflecting on the poor availability of health care services and the poor functioning of the 'follow up' component of the family planning programme in rural areas.

TABLE 2. SYMPTOMS REPORTED AND STATUS OF HELP SOUGHT

Symptoms	Delhi (159 women)				Kumaon (183 women)			
	Reported %	Sought help %			Reported %	Sought help %		
		(Y)	(N)	(NR)		(Y)	(N)	(NR)
Vaginal discharge	31.45	54.00	34.00	12.00	48.63	34.80	57.30	7.90
Tiredness	8.81	35.71	50.00	14.29	62.29	30.70	62.30	7.00
Breathlessness	8.17	46.15	30.77	23.08	44.80	17.10	75.60	7.30
Genital itching/Rashes	5.66	44.44	44.44	11.11	15.85	27.60	72.40	-
Backache	23.89	34.21	57.90	10.53	46.99	22.10	72.10	5.80
Abdominal pain	10.06	37.50	62.50	-	50.27	32.60	60.90	6.50
Vaginal bleeding	-	-	-	-	13.11	16.70	75.00	8.30
Giddiness	11.32	36.84	72.20	-	48.08	17.00	76.10	6.80
Obstetrical problems	-	-	-	-	13.11	29.20	66.70	4.20
Burning during micturition	1.88	33.33	66.67	-	26.77	14.30	77.60	8.20
Prolapse	5.66	44.44	44.44	11.11	6.01	18.20	72.70	9.10
Incontinence	-	-	-	-	14.20	23.10	69.20	7.70
Menstrual problems	24.52	35.90	53.85	10.26	37.15	16.20	77.90	5.90
Pain during intercourse	8.18	53.85	38.46	7.69	22.40	12.20	85.40	2.40

Note: Y = Yes, N = No, NR = No Response.

Among the non-users, the common reasons given for not adopting any measure are: (a) never felt the need; (b) that it is immoral; (c) wanted more children.

A SELECTIVE ANALYSIS OF THE DATA

As stated earlier, the specific questions that we were interested in related especially to the issue of sexual negotiation, unwanted pregnancies, abortion and their interlinkages.

Sexual relations and 'unwanted pregnancies'. Related to sexual negotiation we were mainly interested in finding out the women's reactions when questioned about their ability to refuse sex with their partners. Largely women said that they could refuse sex or say 'no' to their husbands when they wanted, yet questioned about refusing sex while ill or tired, most of them said they would not refuse (Table 4). The set of answers was thus fraught with inconsistencies.

More inconsistencies emerge, when we probe about reactions of their husbands/partners on their refusal. About 50.3 per cent of the women stated that husbands comply; 33 per cent of the women in Delhi

TABLE 3. TYPE OF HELP SOUGHT (%)

Symptoms	Delhi Type of Help			Kumaon Type of Help		
	Govt. Facility	Private Facility	Not Specified	Govt. Facility	Private Facility	Not Specified
Vaginal discharge	14.80	51.40	37.00	45.20	41.90	12.90
Tiredness	40.00	60.00	-	45.70	37.10	17.10
Genital itching/Rashes	-	50.00	50.00	50.00	28.60	21.40
Breathlessness	-	83.30	16.70	25.00	50.00	25.00
Backache	16.67	66.67	16.67	47.40	31.60	21.10
Abdominal pain	16.70	66.70	16.70	56.70	26.70	16.70
Vaginal bleeding	-	-	-	50.00	50.00	-
Giddiness	-	60.00	40.00	40.00	26.70	33.30
Obstetrical problems	-	-	-	71.40	14.30	14.30
Burning during micturition	100.00	-	-	42.90	42.90	14.30
Prolapse	-	50.00	50.00	100.00	-	-
Incontinence	-	-	-	50.00	16.70	-
Menstrual problems	07.14	50.00	42.86	63.60	36.40	-
Pain during intercourse	20.00	60.00	20.00	40.00	40.00	20.00

sample and 38.7 per cent of the Kumaon sample said that their husbands get angry and abusive and can get physically violent; 31 per cent said that the husband's reactions were mixed, sometimes accepting and at time getting violent (Table 5). Thus, although the majority of the women reported an ability to refuse, almost as many reported violent and abusive behaviour of husbands sometimes at least. Clearly, being able to say 'no' is not tantamount to being able to do so without compromising one's basic dignity. One does not know in how many cases the woman could stick on to her refusal. Also, her negative experience in sexual negotiation at any time would surely have shaped her response at later points. Considering the very high reported incidence of violence and abuse by women, their earlier response of being able to say 'no' appears to be more a reflection of a pious wish than indicate any substantive power.

Women can expect little kin support in situations of sexual coercion from husbands. While 78.60 per cent Delhi women would refuse to talk about such eventuality, in 85 per cent of cases in Kumaon, women could expect no familial support. Marital abuse it seems is something that does not usually lead to social sanction of the abuser (Table 6).

Whether women perceived any pregnancy to be 'unwanted' or were unhappy with was another question. In answer, 30.80 per cent of the

TABLE 4. SEXUAL NEGOTIATIONS (%)

Response	Can You Say No Delhi	Kumaon	Ever Say No Delhi	Kumaon	Is It Proper To Say No Delhi	Kumaon
Yes	74.2	42.07	78.6	40.98	78.00	45.35
No	18.9	33.33	13.8	22.95	11.30	18.03
Sometimes	3.8	13.11	3.80	27.86	5.00	30.05
Never thought about it	-	9.28	-	15.84	0.60	-
No information/ No response	3.1	7.10	3.8	7.65	5.70	12.56

respondents in Delhi and 14.20 per cent from Kumaon expressed that they were unhappy with at least one pregnancy at some point in their reproductive life. About 54.70 per cent and 57.40 per cent of women from Delhi and Kumaon said that they had never experienced such unhappiness (Table 7).

Did the women who expressed unhappiness with a pregnancy take any action to terminate it? About 15 out of 49 women from the Delhi sample and 8 out of 26 women from the Kumaon sample said that they continued with the pregnancy. Only a small number (3 in Delhi and 5 in Kumaon) said they had an abortion. Among the others, 18 women in Delhi and 3 in Kumaon said that they had tried to terminate but failed. They tried it on their own or went to a private doctor and were given pills, but termination did not occur (Table 8). About 22.40 per cent of the Delhi sample and 11.50 per cent of the Kumaon sample preferred an abortion but were either advised against it because they were weak, or their families opposed it.

The reasons for a pregnancy being unwanted were: (a) additional work and expenses (22.44 per cent in Delhi; 42.3 per cent in Kumaon); (b) health problems (30.61 per cent in Delhi, 53.84 per cent in Kumaon); and (c) already had enough children (more than 60 per cent in Delhi and 23 per cent in Kumaon) (Table 9).

The salient points that emerge on the issue of sexual relations and 'unwanted pregnancies' are as follows:

— Inconsistencies emerge in the replies. Initially the women claim that they have equitable relationship with their partners but on probing more than 60 per cent also say that they face abuse, both physical and verbal, when they actually refuse to have sex.
— Even though nearly two-thirds of the women report violence

TABLE 5. HUSBAND/PARTNER'S REACTION ON REFUSAL[1] (%)

Husband/Partner's Reaction	Delhi	Kumaon
Would get angry and abusive	22.60	13.60
Would get violent	10.70	25.10
Will accept refusal	39.00	47.00
Others[2]	21.40	9.90
No information	6.30	4.4

Note: 1. There are multiple answers to this question in some cases. Most of these are clubbed under 'others' category, excepting where violence appears as one of the stated reactions, in which case, the entry is clubbed under that point.

2. Others includes cases where men get violent sometimes and accept refusal sometimes.

TABLE 6. FAMILY'S REACTION IF COERCED (%)

Reaction	Delhi	Kumaon
Family will object to coercion	4.40	4.90
Family will not object	16.40	85.80
Can't say	0.60	0.60
No information	78.60	8.70

TABLE 7. PREGNANCY, IF ANY, YOU WERE UNHAPPY WITH? (%)

Response	Delhi	Kumaon
Yes	30.80	14.20
No	54.70	57.40
Can't say	1.30	14.80
No information/No response	13.20	13.60

and abuse in sexual relations, very few admit to having 'unwanted pregnancies'.

— Where women report pregnancies as unwanted, the main cause seems to be that they have had enough children already.

— Among the women who report some pregnancy or the other to have been 'unwanted', about two-thirds report to have had an abortion or tried to have one or desired to have one.

— The question of family support in times of sexual abuse does not arise for some because they were mainly nuclear families (as in the Delhi sample). Women mostly said that disagreements ended up with them giving in. Many of the respondents consider it a very private issue and feel embarrassed to talk about it with others. But from the responses of those who did talk, in case of joint families most of the women could not approach the family at all in cases of abuse.

Induced abortions. Two sets of questions, namely the experience of women who admitted to having an induced abortion and knowledge of other women opting for induced abortion were asked. In the first set of questions pertaining to details about the number and experience of abortions that they had, no information was forthcoming, even from women who had expressed perceiving at least one pregnancy as unwanted and had an induced abortion. They were more willing to talk about other women who had opted for induced abortion.

The initial response of women to the question 'whether having an abortion was quite common in the area' was one of no response (Table 10a). When the question was later rephrased as 'what does a woman do if she finds herself with a pregnancy she does not want', 32.10 per cent (Delhi) and 49.18 per cent (Kumaon) said that she would opt to continue with the pregnancy while 32.70 per cent (Delhi) and 18.09 per cent (Kumaon) said that she would opt for an abortion. The rest either said they did not know or did not respond (Table 10b). To check for inconsistencies in responses, the women were then asked 'are there many women seeking abortion?' The responses were as follows: 35.20 per cent (Delhi) and 8.20 per cent (Kumaon) women said that 'many' women did seek abortion while 23.30 per cent (Delhi) and 43.70 per cent (Kumaon) said that only a few sought to have abortion. The rest either did not respond or said that they did not know what other women did (Table 10c).

The most commonly listed reasons for seeking abortion in both places were for controlling family size and spacing children (40.8 per cent Delhi and 68 per cent Kumaon). An almost equal percentage stated that they did not know why women sought abortion. The rest gave reasons like, in case of rape or incest, if the child would be a girl and to preserve mother's health (Table 11).

On being asked where women normally went for abortion, nearly a third in both samples cited ignorance. Coupled with 'no response' cases, this is a fairly high percentage, suggesting as before, unwillingness to

TABLE 8. WHAT ACTION TAKEN FOR UNWANTED PREGNANCY?

Action Taken	Delhi		Kumaon	
Continued pregnancy	15	(30.60)	8	(30.80)
Had an abortion	3	(6.12)	5	(19.20)
Tried to terminate but failed	18	(36.70)	3	(11.50)
Others*	11	(22.40)	3	(11.50)
No information/Response	2	(4.10)	7	(26.90)

Notes: *Others category includes where they were advised against it because they were weak and family disapproved.
Figures in parentheses indicate percentages.

TABLE 9. REASONS FOR UNHAPPINESS

Causes	Delhi		Kumaon	
Too much additional work	3	(6.12)	5	(19.23)
Too much additional expense	8	(16.32)	6	(23.07)
Health problems	15	(30.61)	14	(53.84)
Too many children	31	(63.26)	6	(23.07)
Others	1	(2.04)	1	(3.84)
No information	-		1	(3.84)

Note: Figures in parentheses indicate percentages.

talk about the issue. Among those who spoke, government facilities—Safdarjung Hospital in the Delhi sample and PHC/ANM/VHW combine in Kumaon—come high up on the list, closely followed by private doctors (Table 12).

Abortion is not an issue most women were ready to see as their right. Few would condone it under most circumstances. Some said that they would advise a friend to opt for an abortion only under special circumstances, especially if she had too many children already. Many others said that under no condition would they advise an abortion because it was morally wrong and children were God's gifts (Tables 13 and 14). Either a government hospital/facility or private facility would be the place where they would advise their friend to go depending on her paying capacity (Table 15).

The salient features that emerge from the responses regarding induced abortion are:

TABLE 10A. IS HAVING AN ABORTION QUITE COMMON IN YOUR AREA?

Response	Delhi		Kumaon	
Yes	11	(6.90)	68	(37.20)
No	7	(4.40)	64	(35.00)
Do not know	12	(7.50)	39	(21.30)
No response	133	(84.20)	12	(6.60)

TABLE 10B. WHAT DOES A WOMAN WITH AN UNWANTED PREGNANCY NORMALLY DO?

Response	Delhi		Kumaon	
Continues pregnancy	51	(32.10)	90	(49.18)
Tries for abortion	52	(32.70)	33	(18.09)
Others	53	(33.30)	53	(28.96)
No response	3	(1.90)	11	(6.01)

TABLE 10C. REPEATED AGAIN: DO MANY WOMEN IN YOUR LOCALITY SEEK ABORTIONS?

Response	Delhi		Kumaon	
Many	56	(35.20)	15	(8.20)
Some	37	(23.30)	80	(43.70)
No response	23	(14.50)	24	(13.10)
Don't know	43	(27.00)	60	(32.80)
Others	-		4	(2.20)

Note: Figures in parentheses indicate percentages.

— The women personally distance themselves from the issue of induced abortion but are willing to talk about other women.
— Equal percentages of women either opt for an abortion or continue with their pregnancy.
— In the Delhi sample most women seem to be using government health services. In the Kumaon sample, it was mainly home remedies and traditional methods. This might be so because of a general paucity of health services in the region.
— Two impressions stand out regarding women advising their friends to opt for an abortion. Those who would advise a friend to opt for an abortion would do so only in case she has had enough (too many) children.

TABLE 11. REASONS FOR SEEKING ABORTION

Reasons	Delhi		Kumaon	
1. For controlling family size	30	(25.15)	82	(44.80)
2. To space children	25	(15.72)	45	(24.59)
3. When pregnant out of wedlock	18	(11.32)	60	(32.78)
4. In case of rape	7	(4.40)	39	(21.31)
5. In case of incest	1	(0.62)	9	(4.91)
6. To preserve mother's health if at risk	11	(6.91)	1	(0.56)
7. If the child will be a girl	15	(9.43)	13	(7.10)
8. Do not know	56	(35.22)	37	(20.21)
9. 1 and 2	30	(18.86)	1	(0.54)
10. No response	15	(9.43)	13	(7.1)

Note: Figures in parentheses indicate percentages.

— Others cannot contemplate ever advising a friend to opt for an abortion because they feel that it is morally wrong and that children are God's gifts.

Gender perspectives. A small section of the questionnaire was canvassed for men from the families from which the women were interviewed. The aim was twofold. First, we wanted to get the men's views on issues affecting women's lives and secondly to cross-check the men's responses against those of their womenfolk. Interesting features emerge from the men's answers, especially when these are mapped against the responses of their womenfolk (see Table 16).

The same question, it may be seen, when addressed to husband and wife can evoke different answers in a large number of cases. Thus, nearly 50 per cent of the Delhi husbands could not tell how many times their wives had been pregnant. The contradictions between the answers of the couples regarding the use or non-use of various contraceptive methods clearly indicate the significant communication gap that exists between the two in the matter.

This apart, the answers to the questions in this section suggest the following conclusions:

— Generally, men feel they have a harder life than the women as they have to go out to earn a livelihood. This is so even in families where the women are engaged in work outside the home.
— When questioned about serious ailments in the family, men tend

TABLE 12. Whom Do They Go to for an Abortion?

Response	Delhi		Kumaon	
No response	23	(14.50)	10	(5.50)
Trained *dai*	1	(0.60)	9	(4.90)
Untrained *dai*	5	(3.14)	6	(3.30)
Private doctor	31	(19.50)	31	(16.90)
PHC	14	(8.80)	58	(31.70)
ANM/LHW	1	(0.60)	72	(39.30)
An older woman in the house	-		5	(2.70)
Neighbours	-		3	(1.60)
Government hospital	36	(22.60)	-	
Home remedies/Traditional methods	1	(0.60)	5	(2.70)
Don't know	45	(28.30)	52	(28.40)
Others	11	(6.90)	10	(5.50)
Dispensary	8	(5.03)	2	(1.09)

Note: Figures in parentheses indicate percentages.

to report their own problems much more frequently. This appears to be less a reflection of the objective state of affairs and more one of perceptions, as can be seen from responses to probing questions on women's health.

— Men's awareness about the health status of their wives is abysmal. The ignorance was more pronounced in case of reproductive health. An alarmingly large number of men from all survey locations were unaware of reproductive health problems that their wives have been suffering from. For many couples, the number of pregnancies reported by the men and women did not tally. The same could be said about miscarriages and induced abortion. The men did not appear to remember the maternal history of their wives.

— Most men interviewed were currently not using any contraceptive device. A very large percentage had never used any. A very small percentage had undergone vasectomy. Many of the men expressed concern about the side-effects of contraception used for themselves, while a significantly smaller percentage expressed similar concern for their wives.

— Most men said that they would not allow their wives to terminate an unwanted pregnancy. The only exception was the Delhi sample, where the men seemed to know all the politically correct answers.

TABLE 13. WOULD YOU EVER ADVISE A FRIEND TO GO FOR AN ABORTION?

Response	Delhi		Kumaon	
Yes	56	(35.20)	13	(7.10)
No	72	(45.30)	124	(67.80)
No response	22	(13.80)	31	(16.90)
Do not know	11	(6.90)	19	(10.40)

TABLE 14. APPROPRIATE SITUATION FOR AN ABORTION

Response	Delhi		Kumaon	
No Response	25	(15.70)	7	(3.80)
In case of rape	13	(8.18)	49	(26.80)
In case of incest	5	(3.14)	33	(18.03)
Pregnancy out of wedlock	14	(8.80)	55	(30.10)
Mother's health seriously at risk	23	(14.50)	51	(27.90)
Too many children already	52	(32.70)	59	(32.20)
Likelihood of another girl	7	(4.40)	15	(8.20)
Never	45	(28.30)	71	(38.80)
Others*	32	(24.10)	10	(5.46)

Note: *Others includes—Husband is not earning/poor.

TABLE 15. WHOM/WHERE WOULD YOU ADVISE THE WOMAN TO GO?

Response	Delhi		Kumaon	
No response	27	(17.00)	33	(18.00)
Trained *dai*	-	-		
Untrained *dai*	-		-	
Private doctor	30	(18.86)	-	
PHC doctor	1	(0.63)	-	
ANM/LHV	-	-		
An older woman in the house	-	-		
Neighbours	-	-		
Government hospital	39	(24.35)	-	
Home remedies	-		-	
Do not know	9	(5.70)	-	
Others	47	(29.60)	9	(4.90)
Abortion is morally wrong	7	(4.40)	1	(0.50)
Dispensary	2	(1.30)	-	
No suggestions	4	(2.50)	140	(76.50)

Note: Figures in parentheses indicate percentages.

TABLE 16. CONTRADICTIONS IN COUPLE RESPONSES

Contradictions	Delhi (%)	Kumaon (%)
Incidence of current illness in the family	54	25
Number of pregnancies the wife has had	48	29
Pregnancy related health problems for wife	62	43
Use of contraceptive devices as reported by men for self:		
(a) None	72	29
(b) Vasectomy	8	12
(c) Condom	16	33
For wife:		
(a) None	64	28
(b) Tubectomy	32	23
(c) IUD	4	32
Contraception-induced health problems		
(a) Can cause problems for self	-	46
(b) Can cause problems for wife	12	29

— A review of the answers reveals a plethora of contradictions that need to be analysed in greater detail.
— There are strongly held views about the duties of men and women among the men. Gender roles are very clearly defined, with the commonly held belief that strong sanctions are required, and justified, for erring wives. Here again, the Delhi men, by and large, appear to be different, although the veracity of their statements needs to be looked into. There are known cases of violent and abusive husbands in this sample who have come out with politically correct answers.
— It would be blatantly wrong to suggest that all men come out as abusive and violent monsters. There are significant differences even within each sample. The general picture that emerges from the men's responses is, however, one of ignorance of, and hence insensitivity towards the problems that women live with, health problems being one of them.

CONCLUDING OBSERVATIONS

The picture that emerges from our reading of the data is that whatever be the nature and extent of choice these women have in reproductive matters, it cannot be adequately defined in terms of clear-cut binary alternatives. The pressures on the woman, both material and otherwise, are often selectively internalized in such a manner such that what may appear to be a potent option to an outsider may simply not be perceived as an option. Thus in spite of the extensive knowledge of contraceptive methods among women from the Delhi sample and the accessibility of medical facilities and services in the vicinity, the actual use of contraception is minimal.

The majority of the surveyed women may also proclaim that they can refuse sex to their husbands, yet in the same breath, two-thirds also report violence and/or abuse on refusal.

Inconsistencies emerge also with regard to the perception of the notion of unwanted pregnancies. Few are prepared to label any of their own pregnancies as unwanted, or to admit going in for induced abortion themselves. Yet a large majority say that abortion is widespread in their vicinity, and mostly used as a method for controlling family size. The nature of constraints which these women labour under becomes clearer when one considers the fact that apart from inadequate services and supplies, there is an appallingly high rate of morbidity among these women, which was revealed on probing about their health, and a near total absence of male support or sensitivity towards female health problems.

NOTES

1. The project titled 'Woman-sensitive Population Policies and Programmes' was funded by the United Nations Fund for Population Activities (UNFPA) at Delhi between August 1993 and March 1995. The questionnaire used for collecting the information analysed in the survey was prepared by ISST and revised in an expert group meeting in July 1994 in New Delhi. We are grateful to the four non-governmental organizations, i.e., SAMPARK in Bangalore, MARG in Delhi, RUPANTAR in Madhya Pradesh and MAHILA HAAT in the Kumaon Hills for fielding the questionnaires. Processing and analysis of the data generated in the survey has been done at ISST. ISST researchers who have contributed to the project at various stages are Pallavi Ghosh, Shilu Ray, Sanjay Chattopadhyay and Ira Singh.
2. This section is based on the qualitative reports submitted to ISST by the collaborating NGOs in the two locations and subsequently included in the final report of Phase II of the project.

REFERENCES

Cain, Mead, 1984. 'Women's Status and Fertility in Developing Countries: Son Preference and Economic Security', World Bank Staff Working Paper No. 682. Population and Development Series number 7, Washington D.C.

Dyson, Tim and Mick Moore, 1983. 'On Kinship Structure, Female Autonomy and Demographic Behaviour in India', *Population and Development Review*.

ISST, 1994. *Listening to Women*, Report on project titled 'Evolving a Woman-Sensitive Population through Consultations with Rural Women in India', ISST/UNFPA, New Delhi.

———, 1995. *Evolving a Woman-Sensitive Population Policy and Programme*, Final Report, ISST/UNFPA, New Delhi.

Jeejeebhoy, S.J., 1991. 'Women's Roles: Health and Reproductive Behaviour' in J.K. Satia and S.J. Jeejeebhoy, *The Demographic Challenge: A Study of Four Large Indian States*, Oxford University Press, Bombay.

Kabeer, Naila, 1992. *From Fertility Reduction to Reproductive Choice: Gender Perspectives on Family Planning*, IDS Discussion Paper, No. 299.

Mason, Karen, 1984. *The Status of Women: A Review of its Relationships to Fertility and Mortality*, The Rockefeller Foundation, New York.

III
NGO Initiatives in Health Care

Women in Panchayati Raj: Implications for Health for All

N.H. Antia and Nerges Mistry

It took fifteen years of medical education and another fifteen years of surgical practice to realize that neither by training nor practice was I (N.H. Antia) capable of understanding the real problems of illness, leave aside of health, that confront the common people of our country. What I had learnt and practised was a ritualistic exercise in medical technology for which patients provided the necessary 'interesting' clinical material. This also provides kudos and lucre. These were three decades of enchantment with Western medical science and technology that had instilled pride and prestige in increasingly narrow disciplines of curative medicine; an exercise which was divorced from the broader medical epidemiological approach leave aside the social, economic, cultural and political factors that determine both health and illness as also medical care. The profession was not only being increasingly isolated from its patients, but also from society at large. It had acquired a strange pride, in its increasingly specialized technical expertise which was borrowed *ad hoc* from the West. Mentally and culturally enslaved by the West, like its mentors, it too derided our indigenous systems of medicine which were based on a more holistic concept of life, and concerned more with health than with mere disease. Some members of the profession even despise their own culture demonstrating the extent of alienation.

The profession as a result has not only failed to utilize the best aspects of our own systems of medicine but has also failed to utilize the best of the Western system. Being imitators they have neither been able to adapt their newly acquired knowledge to the entirely different requirements of our country, nor have they been able to provide an original contribution in their chosen field despite being exposed to one of the largest storehouses of pathology.

Following extensive training abroad, the first brush with native reality was at the Kondhwa Leprosy Hospital in 1958. This was chiefly the result of an intense desire to practise the newly acquired art of plastic surgery on the 'interesting' clinical material provided by the deformities of this disease. Fortunately, this powerful technological urge also helped to overcome not only the fear of this disease but also the almost insuperable hurdles in the undertaking of complicated surgery in leprosarium under conditions which were little better than that of a kitchen, sans electricity, water supply, anaesthetists or trained medical assistance. The inevitable innovations which helped to simplify the complicated, was later to be termed as 'elegance'. This experience also demonstrated the remarkable ability of illiterate and deformed patients to serve not only as stretcher bearers, physiotherapists and nurses but also as surgical assistants. Their enthusiasm and commonsense helped to make up for their medical shortcomings. This also helped me to overcome the popular confusion between education and intelligence and to demystify medicine. And yet, it was only in the early 1970s that the decision was ultimately made to try and understand the problems of those who came from different villages as a last resort to our department in an urban medical college for the correction of severe deformities, many of which could have been prevented or minimized by relatively simple early attention. Two years of week-end observation of the people and of the medical services in a typical rural area of the Konkan across the harbour of Bombay revealed the almost total failure of both public and private health services. The public (PHC) service was almost entirely devoted to achieving family planning targets utilizing ANMs stationed at the subcentres, while a distant district hospital provided curative treatment for dire emergencies. The local BAMS (ayurvedic) doctor indulged in antibiotics and corticosteroid injections for rapid symptomatic relief, regardless of their dangerous long-term effects. As a result, the majority of the people relied chiefly on their own traditional folk remedies and practices. It was also evident that the vast majority of their medical problems were due to communicable diseases whose underlying cause was poverty resulting from centuries of exploitation. And yet, it was remarkable to see how those deprived of education and the most meagre necessities of life could survive using skills which the urban affluent cannot even imagine.

In the absence of any meaningful form of public or private medical care, and not possessing the knowledge or wherewithal to tackle the problem of poverty, it was decided to see whether the available medical knowledge and technology could be utilized by the people themselves for their own welfare in the absence of any alternative. Since the problem of health chiefly affected women and children, 30 women were selected for this experiment, one for every 1,000 population. A highly practical training, mainly in the form of discussion, was conducted for their common problems. This was either under a tree, or at the village well, or on the verandah of a school, or gram panchayat office in full view of the village utilizing local 'clinical' material available in the village as patients. A very modest referral service was provided by a BAMS doctor in the absence of any allopath who would condescend to teach and practise under these conditions.

To our surprise, these semi-literate and even illiterate village women were able to achieve in five years, in the late 1970s, the 'targets' which the government had set for AD 2000 for its own health services for National Disease Control Programmes like diarrhoeal diseases, leprosy, tuberculosis, immunization and even for family planning without any attempt at coercion. These village women immunized the mothers and children and delivered MCH care. They also attended to the village, alerted the community to epidemics, and helped to avert the consequences. Above all, they also proved to be the most effective channel for health education for their community. This was achieved without the coercive 'transfers' and 'target' pressures, and the statistics they collected were accurate. All this at a cost of about Rs 7 per capita per annum.

Aware of the abilities of the village women, the next experiment at Malshiras was designed to see whether, if the people were given such information on health and the public health services, they would be able to achieve similar results. The answer was clearly in the negative, for unlike an NGO, the PHC has little interest in and virtually no accountability to the people that it is meant to serve.

It was also realized that even most NGOs, though motivated to serve the people, also create a sense of dependency rather than of self-help. This is revealed by the fact that these projects seldom sustain themselves when the NGO departs.

The ICSSR/ICMR report of 1981, *Health for All: An Alternative Strategy*, for which FRCH had provided the research as well as the secretarial help had clearly defined health in a far larger dimension as compared to its popular association with illness and health services. This report also indicated that contrary to popular belief, both health as well as medical care are chiefly within the domain of the people's own effort. But this could be achieved only if the people had adequate financial resources at their command as also the administrative and financial control over these resources and services meant for their welfare. This report also clearly indicated that health cannot be achieved in isolation by medical services. Panchayati Raj was, hence, a precondition for health as also for other social and economic activities that rightly belong to the domain of the local community; for health is based on nutrition, education, water supply, sanitation, housing and environment and not merely medical care.

The 73rd Amendment to our Constitution now provides the necessary conditions for the common people to display their hitherto latent abilities for they can now obtain the necessary finances and control for implementing the twenty-nine subjects covered by this amendment. The amendment also provides for one-third reservation for women in panchayat bodies, in order to involve them in the development process. With this in view, we embarked on an experimental project at Parinche in Pune district of Maharashtra. The objective was to explore the role that village women can play in their community's welfare, given their enhanced political representation in local governing bodies.

This experiment also aims at providing practical training, not only in health, but also in areas related to veterinary medicines, non-formal education, rural banking, library and public information service. A part of the training programme conducted at Parinche is supported by a grant from MacArthur Foundation.

Geographically, the Parinche area villages are located on an undulating terrain of Purandar taluka in Pune district where the major occupation of the people is farming. The project covers a population of 30,000 comprising mainly politically powerful Marathas in an economy marked with low level of employment and essential services like education and health.

Structurally, the key functionary at the community level is the Senior *Tai* (aunt) who is trained to become a role model for motivating the people and sensitizing them to health activities. Each Senior *Tai* is further supported by four Junior *Tais*, each serving a population of 250. The training programmes for Senior Tais which are mainly participatory in nature emphasize on developing communication, managerial and leadership skills. Besides this, orientation training is also provided on a frequent basis. Monitoring of training modules is a constant feature of the project.

In the first phase, the *Tais* are trained to handle problems related to respiratory tract infections, gastro-enteritis, fever, wounds, etc. In the second phase, training is imparted to provide emergency medical care in inaccessible areas and handle problems related to reproductive tract infections. As a consequence, the project is building up a referral system as well as a local laboratory that can undertake simple investigations to assist women in getting their health problems diagnosed.

One of the major components of the project is clinical management. Its objective with respect to reproductive health is to assist women in diagnosis and treatment of diseases, offer counselling services, and help them eradicate their fears and misconceptions related to the subject.

In our experiment on dealing with health delivery in the project site, we used the panchayat structure for conscientization of the local women. However, we found that while providing information on Panchayati Raj and the twenty nine subjects covered by it is useful in itself, this is not enough. It is necessary to select suitable women from the village itself, train them in a highly innovative manner, and encourage them to solve their community's problems using simple but effective knowledge and technology together with proper use of available supportive services which would now be under their control. The emphasis has to be on the use of local talent and resources by overcoming the sense of dependency created by the present system. If the resources from the various existing programmes are pooled, they would be adequate if handed over directly to the community for supporting a large number of local women for community action. This would also provide self-esteem and local employment to several million women in the 600,000 villages of our country. These women can be trained for varied activities either as part-time or full-time workers; not like the present 'community volunteers' who are paid a pittance of Rs 50 per month, while those employed in the government service receive excessive emoluments just because they are unionized. These new community workers, paid by and accountable directly to their own community, would find prestige in offering their services which would prove a more effective spur to them to work than mere salary.

The cynicism of the politicians, bureaucracy, professionals and the elite towards the implementation of such a people-oriented system is not only the result of their lack of understanding and faith in our common people, but also due to the fear of loss of their status and lucrative jobs. Also, because it would lead to questioning of this inequitable society and demand accountability from those who are paid to serve the people, the bogey of increased corruption and violence in the villages is only raised to propagate the present order based on corrupt and inefficient leadership installed and supported at each level of our present system of governance.

The answer lies not only in the direct allocation of funds to the panchayats themselves, but what is equally important is to ensure the provision of detailed information of all such funds, programmes and services to all the people through avenues not controlled by those who have a vested interest in withholding it. There are various ways of achieving this, ranging from the mass media to the even more powerful medium of the common people and not subject to surveillance and control. The NGOs and many others interested in liberating the people from the age-old tyranny can also play an important role, as also motivated individuals and leaders who still exist in all sections of our society. Only then can India demonstrate to the world what democracy really means.

Reaching Women Through Children at CINI

S.N. Chaudhuri

The Child In Need Institute (CINI) was founded in 1974 and started its activities by providing services for the treatment and prevention of malnutrition in children. The organization began to operate in a village near Calcutta and later expanded its activities in other villages and slum areas.

Services for children were initially provided through the outpatient services of a private hospital located in south Calcutta. From 1974 till 1980, the services expanded to cover villages and slum centres through a series of under-five clinics and a referral paediatric hospital. In-service training was imparted to child health workers who were locally recruited to provide both curative and preventive health care services. An important activity of CINI's health programme for children has been the establishment of CINI Nutrition Rehabilitation Centre (NRC) where more than a thousand children are rehabilitated with their mothers.

After establishing rapport with the community, the organization spread its activities to include programmes on health, literacy and income generation for poor women. The impact of such programmes improved when women were encouraged to form *mahila mandals*. CINI initiated ante-natal care services at regular intervals. For this purpose, traditional birth attendants, popularly known as *dais* were identified and given intensive training in conducting safe delivery. Based on CINI's experience of working with malnourished children, a new programme for pregnant women to ensure safe motherhood was designed. CINI trained MCH workers, who assisted women to detect and confirm pregnancy as early as possible, and access regular ante-natal care and adequate nutrition to ensure birth weight above 2.5 kg. In all, about 500 women have received the benefits of the programme with the result that the incidence of low birth weight has reduced from the State average of over 30 per cent to 17 per cent.

Through mobilizing the support of women, matters related to women's health including reproductive health, safe motherhood, education, and family planning were also tackled. The issue of girl children was also brought forth at various meetings of *mahila mandals* and a strategy of starting girl-child centres to impart literacy and vocational skills to them was started. CINI also holds village-level workshops regularly to generate awareness on gender discrimination and innovate ways of promoting attitudes in favour of girl children in the community.

Due to the spread of sexually transmitted diseases (STD) in some of the peri-urban areas with established pockets of commercial sex workers, a need emerged to provide community-based sexual health services in those areas. With the help of community volunteers and panchayat members, clinics have been started to provide these services which include counselling and social marketing of condoms to sex workers and others affected with STD.

In addition to health-care activities for women and children, attention is also paid towards uplifting the socio-economic status of poor families. As a result of continuous dialogue in *mahila mandal* meetings, programmes aimed at skill development, raising literacy level among women and extending credit facilities to poor families were identified and implemented. Initiated by *mahila mandals* with the support of the panchayati raj members, local credit groups now operate in the CINI project areas to provide economic and social linkages in order to improve the quality of life of women. Meetings and workshops are held at regular intervals to make village women aware of various government and NGO programmes which provide economic and social benefits.

The CINI health care system is also addressing increasingly the high incidence of gynaecological disorders, nutritional deficiencies and other morbidities among women. Prevention and treatment of reproductive tract infections (RTI) including STD receives top priority in women's health care programme of CINI.

STUDIES CONDUCTED BY CINI

In 1988, CINI opened a family spacing clinic out of the felt needs of the women attending the under-five and ante-natal clinic. A large number of the women were found to be suffering from gynaecological disorders. The importance of assessing the magnitude of the problem and developing suitable interventions became an area of priority for CINI. With the aim of identifying the determinants of poor status of women's reproductive health and designing an appropriate and user-friendly intervention, CINI undertook a study during 1991 and 1993, on gynaecological diseases among rural women. The study was conducted in CINI's project area which included 24 Parganas (south), Bishnupur Block I and II. The study was also expected to focus on the perception, attitude and health-seeking behaviour of the women under study.

A sample of 500 rural women of the reproductive age group (13-45 years) inhabiting eight villages of 24 Parganas (south) was selected for this purpose. The analysis of data revealed that 65.3 per cent of the women had complaints of one or more gynaecological problems and the mean morbidity per woman was 2.00.

A similar camp-based study was conducted in 1990, to provide assistance to the West Bengal government's health sector in understanding the magnitude of the problem in three districts of the state, namely North Dinajpur, South Dinajpur and Malda. The study sample included 315 women in the reproductive age group.

The study revealed that more than 87 per cent of the women had some sort of gynaecological complaints and the mean morbidity per woman was 1.5.

An important dimension of the study was a series of discussions held with personnel at various levels (PHC doctors, chief medical officer of health, block medical officer, auxiliary nurse midwives, *dais*, health workers, indigenous healers, medical practitioners and women's groups) to get an idea of their perception of reproductive health and how best it could be addressed.

MAJOR FINDINGS OF THE STUDIES AND SUGGESTIONS

Weaknesses in the health service component. The studies carried out by CINI have revealed that one of the weaknesses of the health service component is that a woman has no place in it other than as a mother. Discussions with women in the districts indicated an extreme lack of information and knowledge among women regarding health issues which often made them susceptible to superstitions and myths.

The study suggests that, *first*, the health service component needs to be expanded to encompass not only family planning services, but also those which take care of gynaecological diseases. *Secondly*, women need to be educated on matters related to their physiology and made to realize that their gynaecological disorder is a medical problem for which there is treatment available, and not a way of life. *Thirdly,* services need to be sensitive and capable of providing supportive counselling and follow-up services.

Social inequality and power of decision-making. The study indicates that gender discrimination exists at all levels in the family and at all stages. It is always true that within family budgets and constraints, it is the men who get priority because of societal perceptions, thereby getting preferential treatment right from childhood. It has been suggested that awareness programmes on the importance of caring for the girl child should be incorporated into the existing service components. Secondly, the organized groups (women, youth, etc.) and NGOs should be involved as change agents to influence the community and change their attitudes. Experience of involving men in the programmes directly or indirectly has been found to have a greater impact. The concept of involving community people of all levels can also accelerate the process of implementation of any programme.

Sensitivity of women's reproductive health problems. Most women have inhibitions about discussing their gynaecological and sexual problems even within their own groups and carry a number of misconceptions and myths associated with it. Many consider these to be an inevitable part of being a woman. To eradicate fears and misconceptions among women, there is need for initiating discussions with them on issues related to reproductive health, including gynaecological disorders. The use of audio and visual aids is an effective way of disseminating information among the masses. Close monitoring, individual caring of sensitive issues and follow-up of cases by peer groups is suggested as an effective way of developing confidence among the people.

Non-availability of professional, accessible and need-based services. The studies have pointed out that although the government has a massive health service infrastructure, the services are not always need-based, but rather target-oriented. Even if quantification in terms of assessing the performance level is important, it is equally important that quality and need-based services be available at the door-step.

A large number of women are suffering from ailments and there is a high level of ignorance among them regarding the disease consequences. Also, due to the non-availability of services (preventive and curative) at the primary health care level, there is a dire need for strengthening health education and curative services at the local level. At the block level, this component could be integrated with the existing health programmes.

The study also suggests training and involvement of ICDS (Integrated Child Development Services) workers and NGOs who share a good rapport with the community and have close contact with them.

There is need for involving multipurpose workers, ANMs, PHNs, health supervisors in PHCs, to spread information about women's health problems and handle them.

Important Suggestions Emerging out of Discussions with Block Medical Officers, PHC Doctors, ANMs, Rural Medical Practitioners

Expanding family planning services. Family planning services should be expanded to cater to women's reproductive health. Health should be examined and treatment given in necessary cases prior to providing any specific method. Close monitoring and follow-up is important. Reproductive health service should essentially cover women above the age of actual reproduction. There should be a change in policy towards perception of women as primary targets of health care. Women should not be looked upon as only 'mothers' in the MCH programme. Health services should be addressed to women not only during their pregnancy but for their broader reproductive health needs. There should be multiple points of contact to make women aware of their health status and its implications.

Involving personnel from medical field. All persons directly connected with implementation of the programmes should be consulted. These include superintendents of district hospitals, gynaecologists and obstetricians, doctors in charge of the post-partum department, doctors and officials at the block level, social welfare officers in hospitals, nurses, ANMs, MPWs, and others in the health structure. If possible, local practitioners should also be involved.

Upgrading infrastructure for better access. Upgrading of block hospitals and PHCs should be done to enable them to provide comprehensive services according to their level of expertise. Social welfare offices in hospitals may be extended and upgraded so that patients get access to all services available. Post-natal care should be made an integrated part of CSSM which will in turn help reduction of gynaecological problems in future.

Educating and informing women. Women should be provided with basic information about their body and its functions. The Government can use its huge army of workers at various levels for this important work. State-level as well as local NGOs should be involved in working hand in hand in this area. Awareness generation and referrals should be encouraged as a focal point of service component for all NGOs working at the grassroot level.

Providing counselling and follow-up services. Supportive counselling and follow-up services need to be built into reproductive health programmes. Such programmes should also involve both men and women, and emphasis should be given to sensitize and promote male responsibility for availing services for their partners.

Improving the quality of service. Poor women in India, especially in rural areas do not have access to safe abortion services, leading to maternal mortality and also high levels of morbidity. This area is sensitive and many women avail of services from the private sector. It is, thus, important to strengthen and improve the quality of services.

Integrating indigenous system with the existing system. Since traditional healers are part of the rural health system, they should, therefore, be integrated with the health programme. With proper training and orientation, they may act as first contacts in a more responsible manner. There is a possibility that they may admit their own limitations and refer women to appropriate medical centres, if available. In view of the limitations of the Government in terms of management, manpower and finances, efforts could be made to integrate the existing services rather than initiating new ones.

Involving international and national organizations. The existing forums and committees, where governments, international organizations and NGOs are working for a common cause, could be best used for such an integrated approach.

Disseminating information. Educational materials need to be developed by involving the community. Training and orientation courses should be organized for service providers at all levels and for both governmental and non-governmental personnel.

REFERENCES

Bang, R.A., A.T. M. Baitula, Y. Chaudhury, S. Sarmukaddam, G and O. Tale, 1989. 'High Prevalence of Gynaecological Diseases in Rural Indian Women', *Lancet* 1(8629).

CINI, 1994. 'Gynaecological Morbidities among Women of Rural West Bengal', unpublished study report.

——————, 1995. 'Children by Choice and Reproductive Health', unpublished study report.

Datta, K.K., R.S. Sharma, P.M.A. Razak, T.K. Ghosh and R.R. Arora, 1980. 'Morbidity Pattern Amongst Rural Pregnant Women in Alwar, Rajasthan A Cohort Study', *Health and Population Perspective and Issues*, 3(4).

Pachauri, Saroj, 1995. Regional Working Papers, No 4, Population Council.

WHO, 1986. *Maternal Mortality Rates: A Tabulation of Available Information*, Division of Family Health, Geneva.

Rural Women's Social Education Centre, Chengalpattu: Case Study of a Grassroots Organization Working for Health Promotion Through Women's Empowerment

T.K. SUNDARI RAVINDRAN

ORIGIN

Rural Women's Social Education Centre (RUWSEC) is a grass-roots women's organization in Tamil Nadu founded in 1981. The organization evolved from an adult education programme. Women who came together to form the organization were 'dalit' women who were working as adult educators in a pilot project of the National Adult Education Programme (NAEP) initiated in 1978. The adult education project had been influenced by Paulo Freire's philosophy of conscientization. Both as a result of the training and exposure received from working as adult educators, and as a consequence of their experiences as women who were playing an important role in the community for the first time, the women began to question their oppression as poor, dalit women. Conflicts on the domestic front and opposition from the male leadership in their communities, and other concerns such as the need to know more about the many reproductive health concerns they had, led to their meeting regularly as a women's group.

After several months, some of them suggested that the experience of meeting together as women to address gender issues around reproductive health and rights be extended to women's groups in their respective villages. Reproductive health and women's well-being overall was their main focus. This owed itself to the conviction that had evolved from their personal experiences, that women cannot become successful 'change agents' addressing social issues without dealing with the lack of control over their bodies and their lives that they experienced. They felt powerless in their personal lives and needed to start with it, and continue to address it alongside other issues of social concern.

After two years of *ad hoc* meetings and numerous workshops with women in different villages, the group consisting of twelve dalit women and me (I was associated with them in the adult education programme) decided to constitute itself into a women's organization addressing issues related to women's well-being through women's empowerment, working in the twelve villages to which the women belonged. The organization's concern from the very beginning was much broader than illness management.

A PROFILE OF THE POPULATION

The health problems encountered in the communities were a product of their landlessness, their subordination as 'dalits' which led to very poor living and working conditions and lack of access to basic amenities and to schooling and health services. According to the baseline survey done by us in 1989, about 60 per cent of the women belonged to agricultural households that are totally landless. Most of these landless households (80 per cent) did not even own the sites on which their huts stand, while 60 per cent did not own any other productive assets, including livestock. The vast majority of women (85 per cent) did not have even a single year of schooling. Housing conditions are poor. Three-fourths of them live in mud huts with thatched roofs, with only one room inclusive of kitchen. There is little space around the houses. These are crowded together in a locality called the *cheri*, specifically allocated in every village by traditional land tenures for habitation of the 'untouchable' scheduled castes.

The situation of dalits during the late 1970s was one of poverty amidst plenty: perceptible increase in the income of upper-caste landowners, but the landless and marginally landed dalits were largely excluded from this process of 'development'. The situation described above would not be documented in surveys and censuses because the upper-caste section of the village would have access to services and amenities.

The lives of dalit women were characterized by a low age at marriage, high fertility and repeated pregnancies, which not only increased their risk of pregnancy wastage, but also seriously compromised their health and well-being. The under-five mortality rate is 184 per 1,000 births, far higher than estimated figures of 114 for the state. Given this and the high rate of pregnancy wastage, contraceptive prevalence is low at only 24 per cent.

This is exactly half the prevalence rate for Tamil Nadu at 53 per cent. As many as 42 per cent of women had suffered from one or more serious problems related to pregnancy and childbirth, and a third of the women were currently suffering from a reproductive health problem at the time of the survey, and 25 per cent from other health problems, with the two often coinciding in the same person.

The interplay between class, caste and gender discrimination seems to be the lynch-pin in any explanation of women's health problems here. Their story is one of growing up in landless families, eking out a hand-to-mouth existence, joining the wage labour force in early adolescence; married early and under tremendous social pressure to bear children immediately—a typical situation of a high-mortality social group. Inadequate nutrition coupled with heavy manual labour on land and early pregnancy causes high pregnancy wastage, and in turn extends the period of child-bearing to their entire reproductive span. Both the need to have at least three surviving children, and fear of health risks discourages contraceptive prevalence. With increasing age and parity women are at higher risk of obstetric as well as gynaecologic morbidity. They are also more vulnerable to general health problems.

The role of overt gender discrimination is most evident in the case of reproductive tract infections in women, and injuries related to domestic violence. Reproductive tract infections, for instance, were in a number of instances, sexually transmitted. Treatment proved useless since both partners, not just the woman, were required to comply with it. The men did not want to be identified as the source of infection. More tragically, they repeatedly reinfected their wives. Domestic violence was again, both a source of physical injury and psychological distress, the latter being far more serious in that it led to self-neglect by women.

The low priority accorded to women's health is reflected in patterns of health care utilization. The baseline survey indicated that women were permitted trained attendance only for the first delivery or when they are very young, although higher order births are as risky or more. Young women, especially teenagers, did not take any action whatsoever for their illness, while women in their early thirties, and wage workers take some form of action promptly. This is because a few days' immobility to loss of wages in a middle aged woman with several dependent children is unaffordable from the family's point of view. The women themselves consider it imperative to take care of themselves, if only to ensure the family's survival. According to some of the young women interviewed, complaining of health problems and seeking medical attention was risky. Being childless, they were of little value to their marital families and might be sent back to their parental homes if they were seen to be 'sickly'. The husband might even remarry. Thus, it seems that in addition to constraints imposed by poverty, an important main barrier to women's utilization of health services related to how society values them. Education, and even access to money/income play, if at all, a minor role. Another major factor constraining access to health services is the poor quality of services and the inhuman way in which women are treated by a hierarchical and elitist health care system which, in addition, has been obsessed with population control and, above all, did not meet most of women's health needs.

GUIDING PRINCIPLES

The women's group (which formed RUWSEC), most of whose members were agricultural wage labourers, sought to challenge the class, caste as well as gender-based subordination which compromised women's well-being. The three were intertwined inextricably, and the group did not see any way of tackling these one at a time in some order of priority.

The group wanted to demystify the notion that health could be 'delivered' by doctors, and believed that people had to be organized to demand for the fulfilment of conditions that made it possible for them to be healthy. Through health education and awareness-raising programmes seeking to empower women with a sound information base, and through programmes aimed at enhancing their self-confidence and self-image, RUWSEC sought to enable women to initiate self-help at home, to be discriminating and well-informed users of health services, and to feel entitled to good health and care.

Our main strategy for achieving this was the organization of local women into 'sanghams' or associations. Our premise has been that the process of coming together to discuss their problems as women and to demand their health and reproductive rights would encourage them to challenge other dimensions of their subordination as women, wage labourers and dalits. This has indeed been the case, and the 'health issues' addressed through these 'sanghams' have ranged from demands for potable water supply, wage struggles, availability of food through the public distribution system, to violence against women, non-functioning of *balwadis*, and poor services in health subcentres and PHCs.

Over the past fourteen years, our work has extended into very wide range of related concerns, and to many more villages and hamlets: we will soon be working in 100 hamlets in the area.

MAJOR ACTIVITIES

The organization has a wide spectrum of activities which may be divided into the following major categories:

— Community-based action for health promotion through a community health worker, formation of a local women's 'sangham' (association) and leadership training for village women
— Publication and distribution of popular education material on health
— Education and empowerment programmes for adolescents
— Work with men for gender sensitization and on reproductive health issues
— Health education and training for other NGOs and annual health festivals
— Creating an information base on the health of rural poor women
— Action/research projects on specific health problems/interventions
— Running a reproductive health services clinic

Community based action for health promotion. Each hamlet has a local woman trained as a community health worker who has successfully mobilized a core group of women leaders into a women's 'sangham' (association). 'Sanghams' act as pressure groups and catalysts initiating and supporting a wide range of health-promoting activities, be it ensuring that all children are immunized and wells are maintained clean; developing and distributing simple delivery kits to ensure safe home delivery; lobbying with family members for permission for undergoing sterilization (for birth control); negotiating with district officials for installing water taps; or leading strikes to demand better daily wages.

Leadership training of women is carried out through fortnightly meetings in villages, and through inter-village workshops conducted three times in a year, bringing together women from several villages at a time. These inter-village workshops deal with a variety of themes related to their health and their lives, information about the macro-forces affecting their well-being, and also with development of leadership and organizing skills.

We have launched several special campaigns on the basis of priority issues identified from time to time. An ongoing campaign which we have actively led since 1988, is against maternal mortality and morbidity.

We have initiated numerous activities including studies to identify the major problems and the efficacy of interventions. Recently initiated campaigns are on prevention and treatment of STDs and action against violence against women.

A cursory look at our reports and data tells us that we have made an impact in terms of perceptibly altering health-seeking behaviour in many respects, in the community as a whole. Women are better informed about factors affecting their health, and feel better equipped and more confident in dealing with these. Virtually all hamlets have initiated action for protected water supply, and many have succeeded. Women's 'sanghams' have ensured that immunization is demanded and secured, and immunization coverage is above 80 per cent in the project area. Wells are maintained clean, and prompt action ensues in case of signs of an epidemic. Few children get diarrhoea any more, and there have been no deaths from it since adherence to ORT became a way of life. The level of awareness about problems related to pregnancy and birth have increased, and we have recorded an increase in hospital deliveries from a mere 25 per cent to about 49 per cent, between 1989 and 1991. Hospital deliveries of cases 'at risk' have gone up to nearly 80 per cent. More women are initiating self-treatment for RTIs and also seeking medical help. Atrocities against women are rarely left unchallenged, and require no external motivation. Medical abuses and inaction in health centres is reported regularly, and local level action attempted to deal with these.

In terms of change in gender roles, a core group of women in each community have gradually come to play a decision-making role and are being accepted as such. Because of their success in securing basic services for the community and because of their knowledge about health issues, they are consulted as capable women. Many have had the courage to stand up against gender biases. In the upcoming panchayat elections, the largest proportion of women contesting are from villages where we work, and these are all dalit women who are either our workers or active in our 'sanghams'.

Publication and distribution of material on health. We have published more than twenty pamphlets in Tamil on topics such as the concept of primary health care, prevention and treatment of major childhood diseases, immunization, self-care during pregnancy, preparing for a hygienic home delivery, danger signals to pregnancy and birth that call for immediate attention, reproductive tract infections, sixteen detailed pamphlets on various methods of birth control including the rhythm method, cervical cancer, breast self-examination, self-care for prevention and treatment of nutritional anaemia, and so on. Four recent books published are *Understanding Our Bodies* and the other, an adapted Tamil version of *Child Birth Picture Book, An Analysis of the Health Care System from the Perspective of Rural Poor Women,* and *A Guide to Allopathic Drugs.*

Education and empowerment programmes for adolescents. This is a programme initiated in 1991, addressed to unmarried adolescents between 11-18 years of age. More than 70 per cent of them were illiterate and working as agricultural labourers. In addition to providing literacy skills, overall personality and assertiveness development, learning about their bodies and responsible sexuality is a very important part of the project.

This programme currently caters to 163 learners who attend regular classes in their respective villages, and 34 learners who are preparing to appear for Class VIII examinations in December 1995.

Gender sensitization workshop for men. Our decision to work with men was a consequence of a growing realization that we were reaching an impasse *vis-à-vis* our attempt at empowering women. Changing expectations and women's unwillingness to put up with subordination was accentuating marital conflicts, and often leading to increasing domestic violence. Also, in the area of reproductive decision-making, while we had worked at enabling women to take informed decisions, their partners knew very little about these issues, and this again was giving rise to conflicts.

Yet another reason was the awareness of growing reproductive health problems and infections among women, as a direct consequence of men's promiscuity. More than a decade of work with women had given us confidence that we could work with men without undermining the cause of women. We began with unsure steps, with workshops for the husbands and relatives of RUWSEC's workers, and also initiated village-level work in collaboration with men from a village-based organization during 1993-4.

Health education training for NGOs. Bi-annual seminars/workshops are organized regularly for women activists from organizations involved in issues other than health to sensitize them to women's health issues.

We reach out to an audience of about five to ten thousand men and women, through our annual health festivals, which consists of a health exhibition, film and video shows, cultural programmes, and sale of publications.

We have a programme of training on gender, health and development for four NGOs in Chengalpattu district, covering both men and women from villages. This consists of a series of seven workshops each.

Information base on the health of rural poor women. In an attempt to make known the health problems of rural poor women and have their voices heard outside, as well as to help us better understand the patterns of illness and factors influencing these across villages so that we can plan better interventions, we initiated a process of creating and maintaining a database on the health of women and children in 1989. A baseline survey was conducted in 48 hamlets and information has been consistently updated on an ongoing basis till today.

The most important aspect of this experiment is that the research process as well as consolidation of data is done by our senior health workers, whose field experiences make their interpretation of data valuable and closer to the truth. In addition to using these for regular planning and monitoring, the information is used in health exhibitions in annual health festivals, and as discussion points in village level 'sangham' meetings.

Action research projects on specific health problems/interventions. In addition to the above, we have undertaken a number of action/research studies in the community related to the usefulness of specific health interventions such as distribution of the safe delivery kit and health education during pregnancy. More recently, we carried out a series of FGDs (focus group discussions) in villages to record women's critique of the population control programme and their agenda for change. This, as well as discussions from a workshop with activists has been widely publicized by us locally and has also been printed recently in the *Radical Health Journal*.

We have also carried out a study on the quality of services provided in primary health centres, in which several NGOs from Tamil Nadu participated. The method adopted was one of participant observation, where activists went in as patients, and made observations, with a checklist as guideline. Sixteen health facilities were studied, and this was further extended by RUWSEC's workers to cover all PHCs in Chengalpattu district.

We have collaborated with other organizations and researchers to study some key issues in the area of reproductive health. These include Users' Perspective Studies on Norplant Acceptors in Madras who were part of the introductory trial, and an experimental intervention in introducing diaphragms in three slum areas located in Madras. Both these have important lessons to offer.

Reproductive health services clinic. As a result of our health-related activities, we have seen a perceptible increase in the level of awareness among women about their health problems, and so also willingness to seek medical assistance. This has created an overwhelming demand for medical help. Besides providing basic care at the community level through the community health worker, our policy so far has been to direct the women to the government's health services—the primary health centres and the referral hospital in the district headquarters. This was guided by the notion that we should not be duplicating services already provided by the public health services. After nearly a decade and a half, we seemed to have reached an impasse because our efforts at organizing were limited to local issues and did not bring about lasting changes: when one PHC doctor went and another came, for instance, we would start all over again. Discussions in 'sanghams' made it clear that it was imperative at this juncture to provide an alternative facility for meeting women's health needs, even while we work at lobbying and pressuring for changes in the existing health services system. This gave rise to the reproductive health services clinic which was started in June 1995. It provides outpatient services for all health problems, but specializes in reproductive health care for women and men. It strives to put into practice our women's dream of the kind of health facility they would like to see, which has shaped the design of this project and is continuously being reviewed. We will soon be providing MTP, delivery and sterilization facilities as well as minor gynaecological surgical procedures. We have a well-equipped laboratory in the clinic. Services and drugs are subsidized.

SOME REFLECTIONS ON OUR STRENGTHS AND LIMITATIONS AS AN ORGANIZATION

Day-to-day working of RUWSEC is entrusted with a Coordinating Team consisting of coordinators of the various projects. The coordinators as well as supervisory staff are all local women who were founding members or others who joined as village-level workers and the way they combine commitment with competence is a matter of great pride to us. They have been trained, through their actual participation in these processes, in programme planning and management, time planning, budgeting and monitoring finances, and taking crucial and sensitive administrative decisions. Our motto has been that no skill or responsibility is beyond someone who is willing to learn, and committed. We continue to make an effort to offer further challenges to those who have the potential among those who have recently joined the team as health or literacy animators.

We also have a Workers' Council, constituted of a number of operational committees—one for monitoring the budget and finances, one for innovative programme planning, one to look into staff performance, another to investigate staff grievances and take decisions (within the limitations imposed by the budget provisions, and one to mediate in village-level problems that may arise from time to time. Representatives are elected from every section of workers irrespective of position or number of years of experience. This gives everyone an exposure to all aspects of running and developing an organization, allows a free airing of views, and maintains a high level of motivation.

We see this as our major strength, but it has not been without some limitations. As an organization headed by local poor women it has remained low profile, and not had the ears of the powers-that-be, to be able to influence policy in a significant way. The women, given their responsibilities at home, have mostly been unable to travel and participate in meetings and events outside the area, and this has limited their experiences and exposure. Their sharing of ideas and learning from other groups has been constrained by their limited knowledge of English, which makes active participation in seminars difficult even when they have tried it. We are working on finding ways of dealing with each of these.

RUWSEC has been funded by foreign donors after the first two years of its existence, and continues to do so. The local communities were too poor to support the women workers, and the dalit women felt that voluntarism was a luxury which middle-class women like me could afford but was not something they could consider. We try as much as we can to keep to the basic needs and requirements. This comes easy to the women who are running it, given their experience in managing tight household budgets.

Dependence on external funding has, however, never to date meant altering a project to suit the donors' needs. We have, at times, said 'no' to further funding because we felt constrained by the donor's expectations, and struggled along. We have also never compromised on our stand that we should have the freedom to be flexible and alter the course of projects in accordance with feedback from the community even if it has narrowed the field for us.

We have been unable to become financially self-sufficient, and this does not seem like a possibility in the near future. The women running the organization are, however, self-sufficient in designing, managing and implementing new and innovative programmes that reflect the priorities and concerns of their communities.

We believe that this will, above all, be the organization's most lasting contributions to the local community—the fact of having tapped and nurtured local women's leadership to take charge of an organization and to develop it imaginatively.

IV
Policy Issues

India's Augean Stables: The Unfinished Health Agenda

MOHAN RAO

This paper attempts to provide an overview of the development of health and family welfare services in India; and in doing so, hopefully provide some insights into the problems that confront us. The paper is divided into two sections. The first traces the evolution and growth of health and family welfare services over the various Plan periods. Stemming from this, the second provides selected data on health indices in the country at present in order to raise issues for discussion.

India's rush to her post-colonial tryst with destiny came encumbered with a host of problems. Chief among them was the widespread and deep poverty in the country reflected in her death and disease profiles. In 1943, the Government of India appointed the historic Bhore Committee to survey the health situation in the country and make recommendations for the future. Remarkably influenced by the considerations of the Beveridge Committee in England which gave birth to the National Health Service in that country, and, equally, by the extraordinary advances in health made in the Soviet Union, the Bhore Committee made far-reaching recommendations guided by two overriding principles. First, the provision of health care services was the responsibility of the State. Second, comprehensive health care should be available to people irrespective of their ability to pay. The blueprint for the development of health services that was outlined, both in the short term and long term, emphasized preventive services, focusing on rural areas and linking health with overall development. These recommendations were considered eminently feasible; indeed they were the minimum irreducible if a dent was to be made in the 'dark shadows' that was the health picture of the country.

The Government of India accepted the recommendations of the Bhore Committee. Yet in the First Plan itself it is noted that out of the total expenditure contemplated, more than half would be for the development of hospitals and dispensaries and nearly 40 per cent of the 'total provision will be for medical education and training'. Primary health centres (PHCs) were to be developed as part of the Community Development Programme. In addition, the First Plan gave birth to the launch of what are called unipurpose, vertical programmes for the control of malaria, smallpox, filaria, leprosy, cholera and venereal diseases.

India was the first country in the world to launch a family planning programme during this period. While recognizing the importance of maternal and child health (MCH), this was to form an integral component of the general health services.

Acting as midwife for both the Malaria Control Programme and the Family Planning Programme were international agencies. Both programmes were premised on the belief that there were technological solutions to complex epidemiological problems: a 'magic bullet' approach that had no historical or indeed, contemporary precedents. Let us recall that malaria receded from Europe as she completed her public health and sanitary revolutions; and that following these, the birth rate declined in these countries in the face of opposition from both the State and religion and in the absence of reliable contraceptive technologies.

The Malaria Control Programme met with phenomenal, and as it turned out, deceptively short-lived success. In the Second Plan, encouraged by international agencies, the control programme was converted into the National Malaria Eradication Programme. It was envisaged that malaria would be eradicated by 1966. The operational strategy for the family planning programme over the first two Plan periods, again inspired by international agencies, was the Clinic Approach.

During the First and Second Plan periods, health obtained 3.3 and 3 per cent of the total outlays respectively. This was well below the irreducible minimum of 10 per cent recommended by the Bhore Committee. To further set a pattern for the future, within this budget, 55 to 60 per cent was allocated to curative health services and medical education. Public health, the lowly daughter of twentieth-century medicine, obtained a mere third. Of the funds available for public health, the vast share was garnered by the vertical programmes—at this point in time primarily malaria and smallpox. Two consequences logically unfolded: while hospitals and medical colleges came forth, PHCs did not.

The Third Plan witnessed the coming to the fore recommendations of the Health Survey and Planning Committee, known in popular parlance as the Mudaliar Committee. The Mudaliar Committee noted that the primary health care system that had evolved so very haltingly, bore no resemblance to that visualized by the Bhore Committee. The committee, pleading a paucity of funds, therefore, recommended that further opening of PHCs be disbanded. Instead, it recommended the upgradation of existing services. The committee noted that only 'when facilities in regard to personnel, finance and other requirements are sufficiently enlarged can the Bhore Committee formula for PHCs be adopted'.

This period saw a flurry of activity in the health sector. In 1962, possibly inspired by the early successes of the National Malaria Eradication Programme, was launched the National Smallpox Eradication Programme expecting fructification within three years.

In 1962 was also launched a programme with a difference: the National Tuberculosis Programme (NTP), the only major communicable disease programme that was based on epidemiological data and was integrated into the general health services. In view of the early success of the NMEP, the Chaddha Committee drew attention to the essential requirements of a general health service system that had to be developed for the NMEP to enter into the Maintenance Phase.

The Third Plan also saw the family planning programme take wings. Alarmed by the results of the 1961 Census which showed a higher rate of population growth than had been anticipated, the Clinic Approach was abandoned in favour of the Extension Education Approach in what was called the Reorganized Programme, again at the behest of international agencies. It was this which gave a fillip to the development of health infrastructure in the country. However, even before the Extension Approach could find its feet, on the recommendation of the United Nations Advisory Mission, it was abandoned in favour of a Reinforced Programme emphasizing IUCDs. The official imprimatur to this policy was provided by the Mukherji Committee Report which also recommended specific targets and incentives. Concerns in family planning came to increasingly shape the development of health services. The UN Advisory Mission also recommended the delinking of MCH from family planning services.

'This recommendation', it noted, 'is reinforced by the fear that the programme may be otherwise used in some states to expand the much needed and neglected maternal and child welfare services.' ANMs were thus to be 'relieved from other responsibilities such as maternal and child health and nutrition' in order to concentrate their activities on family planning.

The increasing demand for both finances and human power emanating from the vertical programmes led to the establishment of another committee for the reorganization of health services. While the Mukherji Committee noted the need for an integrated health service system, it recommended that the family planning programme should continue to have a separate identity as it had 'yet to become, in actual operation, a crash mass programme'.

During the Third Plan, health obtained 2.63 per cent of the total allocation. The allocation to family planning shot up to Rs 50 crore as against Rs 65 lakh in the First Plan and Rs 5 crore in the Second Plan.

All these initiatives notwithstanding, the Fourth Plan document noted that the Malaria Eradication Programme had received setbacks since 1963; that smallpox eradication had not been achieved as anticipated; and that the IUCD programme had met with a 'temporary setback as a result of reported side-effects like bleeding and pain'. Among other reasons—epidemiological, technical and administrative—one of the major causes for the failure of these programmes was that by concentrating on vertical programmes, the general health service system had not been developed.

What started as a trickle of a setback in the NMEP during the Third Plan became a veritable flood in the Fourth, as there was an upsurge of malaria all over the country. Incidence of malaria reached a plateau between 1971 and 1976; and from 1974 onwards, deaths due to malaria started increasing. While the number of cases declined subsequently, the toll of malarial deaths continued to increase remorselessly.

Following a series of smallpox epidemics, an entirely new approach was adopted in the smallpox eradication programme. This finally started paying dividends although when India finally eradicated smallpox in 1975, it had not only poured in much more resources than had been anticipated, draining thereby the budget for the development of health infrastructure, but also earned the country the dubious distinction of being one of the last countries in the world to eradicate this disease. In parenthesis it may be noted that the eradication of smallpox was possible because of the epidemiological uniqueness of the disease; it was this epidemiological understanding that contributed to its conquest.

Despite the note of cautious optimism sounded by the Fourth Plan document, the IUCD programme never recovered from the 'temporary setback'; it was quietly abandoned in favour of mass vasectomy camps. These camps, pioneered in Kerala, were conducted with much fanfare and the financial support of a host of international aid agencies. The pace of the family planning programme was substantially accelerated: family welfare centres for vasectomy were supplemented by more than

1,000 mobile service units. In 1972-3, sterilizations reached a peak of 3.1 million, two-thirds of these performed in camps. At a camp in Gorakhpur in 1972, 11 vasectomized men died of tetanus. By the following year, the sterilization figures were down to 0.94 million and the Department of Family Planning was forced to abandon the camp approach. In view of the inability of the vertical programmes to achieve their goals, there were renewed demands emanating from all of them calling for further increases in finances and staff. Considering this 'disquietening', a committee was appointed to consider the question of integration of the vertical programmes.

The Kartar Singh Committee felt that integration would be economical, effective and feasible and went on to recommend that workers of only four programmes, viz., malaria, smallpox, trachoma and family planning be integrated and designated as multipurpose workers. This vision of integration was seriously flawed: it not only confined itself to a few programmes, it also confined itself to the periphery alone. This left the programmes effectively vertical at the more crucial central levels where priorities were set and financial allocations made. During the Fourth Plan, the budget for health had further shrunk while that for family planning had risen. Health obtained Rs 433.5 crore while family planning garnered Rs 315 crore representing 2.12 and 1.76 per cent of the total outlay. Towards the end of the Plan, it is remarked that things looked gloomy for the family planning programme. It would not be an exaggeration to state that things looked dismal for the health programmes as well. At the same time, there was a growing awareness among international agencies of the failure of the family planning approach to the problem of poverty. Some of the disenchanted argued for more coercive forms of population control, while others called for redirecting development benefits to the impoverished to hasten their adoption of small-family ideals.

Indeed, the World Bank and the Population Council endorsed this 'developmentalist' perspective. The echoes of such shifts reverberated in India as the Fifth Plan codified this changed perspective. It noted that 'the primary objective is to provide minimum public health facilities integrated with family planning and nutrition for vulnerable groups'. The Minimum Needs Programme (MNP), it averred, would be 'the first charge on the development outlays under the health sector'.

The outlay for family planning was increased to Rs 516 crore; health obtained Rs 797 crore representing 0.96 and 1.49 per cent of the total outlay respectively. The Plan committed itself to improving health care services in rural areas through extending the infrastructure under the MNP and integration of the peripheral staff of all the vertical programmes.

The year 1975 enters the annals of the history of public health in India for two reasons. First, in this year India was finally declared smallpox free. Second, the year witnessed the declaration of Emergency which facilitated the passage of the draconian National Population Policy of April 1976 which called for a 'direct assault' on the population problem. A host of anti-natalist measures were announced: central budgetary transfers were tied to family planning programme performance; representation to Parliament was frozen on the basis of the 1971 Census and so on, even as disincentives at the individual level were announced. While nation wide compulsory sterilization was ruled out 'for the time being' due to the lack of health infrastructure, state governments were permitted to do so if they felt the 'time was ripe'.

The direct assault did achieve targets, but sterilizations themselves took a ghastly toll of 1,774 deaths. Largely due to the 'excesses' under the family planning programme, the government was swept out of power in the elections of 1977. The new government announced a family planning programme on a wholly voluntary basis, as an integral part of a 'comprehensive policy' covering education, health, MCH and nutrition.

Meanwhile, the continuing debacle with the NMEP compelled the government to initiate a new approach. The Modified Plan of Operation was announced in 1977 to prevent deaths from malaria and to reduce the morbidity due to it; the goal of malaria eradication was postponed indefinitely.

In 1977, the government announced the implementation of the recommendations of the Shrivastava Committee as a scheme for strengthening rural health care services. The Shrivastava Committee had—as was soon to become familiar—trenchantly criticized the 'western' model of health services that had been adopted in the country as it called for deprofessionalization of health care. The Community Health Volunteers Scheme, thus inaugurated in 1977 as a step towards repositing 'people's health in people's hands', was simultaneously visualized as a scheme for tackling the population problem 'on a war footing'.

Meanwhile, widespread international disillusionment with vertical programmes, recognition of the need to provide sufficient coverage to rural populations, and the faltering integration of preventive and promotive programmes achieved so far, together contributed to the WHO-UNICEF declaration of 'Health For All Through Primary Health

Care' at Alma Ata in 1978. Indeed at this point, the WHO saw a 'major crisis on the point of developing' in both the developed and the developing world as a result of the 'wide and deep-seated error in the way health services are provided'.

The PHC approach emphasized accessibility, affordability, comprehensiveness, integration and, above all, the subordination of health technology to the needs of the people. Inter-sectoral linkages, equity, basic needs and people's participation were seen as the central instruments. This approach, described as revolutionary, was however given short shrift. International agencies were quick to adopt the dubious and singularly ill-christened Selective Primary Health Care approach. It was argued that the PHC approach was too costly, too idealistic and ignored the quick results that could be achieved through the application of simple, cost-effective technologies to selected health interventions.

Although India was a signatory to the Alma Ata declaration, this consideration barely informs the Sixth Plan document. The implementation of the CHV scheme, the MPW scheme, the ROME scheme and the Expanded Programme of Immunization were considered adequate tributes to the PHC approach.

In 1980 was published an important study conducted by the ICMR and the ICSSR entitled 'Health For All: An Alternative Strategy'. It noted:

Within the health sector, our most important recommendation is that the existing exotic, top-down, elite oriented, urban biased, centralized and bureaucratic system which over-emphasizes the curative aspects, large urban hospitals, doctors and drugs should be replaced by an alternative model of health care services. This alternative would be strongly rooted in the community, provide adequate, efficient and equitable referral services, integrate promotive, preventive and curative aspects, and combine the valuable elements in our culture and tradition with the best elements of the western system.

These statements, as well as the recommendations of the Working Group on Population Policy find not too much resonance in the Sixth Plan. The Plan adopted, as per the latter, the long-term demographic goal of reducing the net reproduction rate of one by all the states of the country by 2001. Towards this end, it recognized the need for poverty eradication, improvements in infant and child survival, female literacy and nutrition.

All the principled admission of the need for integration notwithstanding, sectoral allocations continued. The outlay on family planning was again increased to Rs 1,010 crore, and, health obtained Rs 1,821 crore out of a total Plan outlay of Rs 97,555 crore, representing 1.03 and 1.80 per cent of the total budget respectively. The augmenting of rural infrastructure under the MNP received some impetus: the share of MNP in the health budget rose from 17 per cent in the Fifth Plan to 31 per cent in the Sixth. However, this was at the relative cost of preventive health programmes, for the reduction in medical infrastructure was only 4 per cent, whereas that for the control of communicable diseases was 11 per cent.

At the same time, this Plan also saw official imprimatur to the increasing entry of the NGO and the private sector in health care, the latter fattened with subsidies and tax benefits. While the Health Policy enunciated during this period echoes the criticism made by the ICMR-ICSSR Committee, it does not concretely address the problems that it recognizes. On the other hand, its perspective is entirely within that of the vertical programmes as it accords 'very high priority' to family planning, control of leprosy, tuberculosis and blindness. It refers not to universal primary health care but to 'primary health facilities on a universal basis'.

During the Sixth Plan period, in keeping with the suggestion of the Working Group on Population Policy, there was an increasing emphasis on the sterilization of women, often at laparoscopic camps. Health programmes that were included in the Twenty Point Programme, viz., tuberculosis, leprosy and UIP were now assigned targets to be achieved while the CHV scheme was unceremoniously buried. In a move staggering the epidemiological imagination, the Plan set up, as one of its goals, the eradication of leprosy by AD 2000 through recourse to multi-drug therapy regimes.

While the Seventh Plan notes the inability to meet the targets set out both for rural infrastructure development and control of communicable diseases in the Sixth, it sees no contradiction in recommending the 'development of specialities and super-specialities' to grapple with the 'major health problem of non-communicable diseases'. These were identified as cancer, coronary heart diseases, hypertension, diabetes, rheumatic heart disease, traffic and other accidents; and pilot projects for their prevention and control were initiated. 'Voluntary organizations and other private institutions' were to play an increasing role.

During this period, the National AIDS Control Programme commenced with a 'soft loan' of US$84 million from the World Bank and technical assistance from the WHO. A separate organization, the NACO, was consequently set up. In its review of the family planning programme in the preceding Plan period, the Seventh Plan document observed that achievements fell short of expectations in all the components of the programme. The performance of the MCH component in the field of immunization and antenatal care, despite the UIP and the GOBI-FFF approaches, were 'far from satisfactory'. In addition to recommending the strengthening of the infrastructure and the vigorous implementation of the programme with particular reference to the poorly performing northern states, the Plan stressed the need to pay greater attention to MCH activities to enhance child survival. These concerns, along with the commitment to promote a two-child norm as a 'vital means to the attainment of the goal of Health For All in the shortest possible time', find expression in the National Population Policy of 1986. The allocation to family planning again increased, to be almost on par with that for health. Family planning and health obtained Rs 3,256 crore and Rs 3,392 crore out of a total outlay of Rs 1,80,000 crore, representing 1.80 and 1.88 per cent respectively.

Despite these efforts, it was increasingly, albeit grudgingly, being accepted that the programme had reached a dead-end. The mid-term appraisal of the Plan notes that 'a recent report of the Registrar General based on SRS data indicates that the birth rate has not fallen' despite the couple protection rate having increased considerably. This was echoed by the Public Accounts Committee in its 139th Report.

The Eighth Plan document again notes the depressingly familiar inability to meet the goals of the previous Plan in control of communicable diseases, in achieving the family planning goals and, indeed, in being able to build basic infrastructure. It notes that the backlog of Sub-centres, PHCs and CHCs 'is staggering and the resources required ... astronomical and as such unachievable' and, therefore, recommended consolidation rather than expansion. It also committed itself 'to encourage private initiatives, private hospitals/clinics' for secondary and tertiary care even as it noted that 'it is time that the concept of free medical care is reviewed and people are required to pay, even if partially for the services'. The allocation to health was Rs 7,572 crore and to family planning Rs 6,500 crore, again indicating where priorities lay.

During this period, AIDS control began to assume increasing importance, not so much because it was assessed as a major public health problem epidemiologically, but because funds began flowing from international agencies. The NTP, which in a memorable phrase, had been designed to 'sink or sail' with the general health services, meanwhile, came in for scrutiny. This was not compelled by the morbidity and mortality caused by the disease which relentlessly continued, but by the association of this disease with AIDS. The NTP had sunk because the general health services were not allowed to stay afloat. Instead of strengthening the general health services, international agencies advocated a short-term chemotherapy regime based on more expensive second-line drugs for which loans now became available. This is not an approach epidemiologically assessed as cost-effective, nor likely to be one that our country can afford. But once again an approach based on medical technology alone garners centre stage.

Meanwhile, the reforms under the structural adjustment programme embarked upon by the government in the Eighth Plan have involved further withdrawal in India's commitment to health sector development. The central grants as a proportion of the State's total medical and public health expenditure fell sharply. In the case of centrally sponsored disease control programmes, the share of central grants declined from 41 per cent in 1984-5 to 29 per cent in 1988-9, and sharply to 18.5 per cent in 1992-3. Real expenditure, obviously, declined even more sharply. The states with a high degree of dependence on the Centre, the poorer states, which are also precisely the states with poor development of social sectors, suffer more when central grants are cut. The real expenditure in these states declined on all items of health sector in general and in public health in particular. Table 1 presents the relevant data.

The family planning programme is once again at the cross-roads. It is in this context that the Expert Group on Population Policy endorses 'newer hormonal contraceptives for women' on the argument that no medication is free from side-effects. It is in this context too that the World Bank calls for a new 'reproductive and child health approach' to give a new lease of life to a programme in the doldrums. What the reproductive health approach does, is completely miss the epidemiological wood for the trees. Even within the reproductive age group of women, among the causes of death, those related to reproduction form a very small proportion indeed. Ignoring this salient fact, while refurbishing this programme, would be yet another red herring which India can ill afford.

It would be churlish indeed to deny the health achievements since independence. The foregoing, however, offers us, in short, two significant lessons. First, that planning in health has not always been influenced by epidemiological considerations. Health programmes have often been initiated without an understanding of the nature of diseases, their distribution, their causes, their behaviour over time and interlinkages,

TABLE 1. SHARE OF CENTRAL GRANTS IN STATE'S HEALTH EXPENDITURE (%)

Year	Medical and Public Health	Public Health	Control of Diseases	Family Welfare
1984-5	6.73	27.92	41.47	99.00
1985-6	6.16	26.29	41.51	92.12
1986-7	4.98	21.70	33.37	90.23
1987-8	4.65	21.39	31.60	89.39
1988-9	4.24	19.83	29.12	90.89
1989-90	3.91	16.66	n.a.	74.51
1990-1	3.21	15.24	24.43	81.72
1991-2R	3.50	15.72	25.21	72.31
1992-3B	3.70	17.17	18.50	88.59

Source: Tulasidhar, V.B., 'Expenditure Compression and Health Sector Outlays', *Economic and Political Weekly* 28(45), 1993.

and indeed, often even their quantum. Above all, they have been guided by technological determinism.

Second, it is politics which determines which among the problems is selected for intervention. In other words, given that diseases and deaths are distributed as unevenly as resources, it is politics which contours the nature and content of interventions and not epidemiologically assessed needs and priorities. Indeed, this limits the possibilities of the very interventions that are adopted. It is, thus, that we have health indicators today telling us a rather sorry tale. Table 2 presents the data on the infant mortality rates in the major states by rural-urban distribution.

While Kerala has achieved an IMR on par with developed countries, states such as Madhya Pradesh, Orissa and Uttar Pradesh continue to have rural infant mortality rates running into three figures. The data on infant mortality rates indicate then that these are still unconscionably high. In addition, they draw attention to the marked interstate and rural-urban differentials.

Table 3 presents the data on the proportion of child deaths in the population by major states, again by rural-urban distribution. The data here reveal the continued high preponderance of child deaths in all the major states of India with the singular exception of Kerala. Indeed, in some states such as Madhya Pradesh, Uttar Pradesh and Rajasthan, they account for close to half the total deaths in the population. This clearly tells us that India is yet to undergo a health transition or epidemiological transition.

TABLE 2. INFANT MORTALITY RATE AMONG THE MAJOR STATES
BY RURAL URBAN DISTRIBUTION (PER 1000 LIVE BIRTHS)

State	Rural	Urban	Combined
Andhra Pradesh	73	56	70
Assam	78	39	76
Bihar	77	46	75
Gujarat	79	54	72
Haryana	73	53	69
Himachal Pradesh	n.a.	n.a.	n.a.
Jammu & Kashmir	n.a.	n.a.	n.a.
Karnataka	80	39	70
Kerala	17	15	17
Madhya Pradesh	120	61	111
Maharashtra	64	44	58
Orissa	127	68	122
Punjab	66	45	61
Rajasthan	88	59	84
Tamil Nadu	70	37	59
Uttar Pradesh	105	67	99
West Bengal	68	41	63
All India	86	50	80

Source: Government of India, CBHI, Health Information of India, New Delhi, 1992.

Table 4 presents the data on the causes of deaths by major cause groups in rural India.

Notwithstanding the crude categorization adopted, what the data make arrestingly clear is that there has been no change in the pattern of mortality. The diseases of poverty and under-nutrition which underlie most of the categories mentioned in Table 4, continue to be the largest causes of death. This is further substantiated by the data on communicable diseases. Over the last several years, there has occurred what has been described as an 'epidemic of epidemics'. There have been epidemics of cholera and gastro-enteritis, Japanese encephalitis, kala-azar and cerebral malaria. Accompanying the upsurge of communicable diseases was the notorious plague epidemic which brought the dismal state of public health into glaring limelight. Table 5 presents some of the relevant data.

Table 6 presents some salient data on the nutritional situation in the country.

TABLE 3. PERCENTAGE OF CHILD DEATHS IN THE MAJOR STATES BY RURAL URBAN DISTRIBUTION

State	Rural	Urban	Combined
Andhra Pradesh	32.09	29.01	31.63
Assam	42.68	27.74	41.94
Bihar	46.31	37.80	45.77
Gujarat	36.29	30.53	34.84
Haryana	44.29	34.71	42.62
Himachal Pradesh	32.92	21.53	32.50
Jammu & Kashmir	39.77	31.23	38.51
Karnataka	36.11	26.70	34.10
Kerala	12.27	14.32	12.66
Madhya Pradesh	51.02	39.51	49.50
Maharashtra	33.27	26.88	31.55
Orissa	39.54	33.28	39.19
Punjab	31.03	27.22	30.15
Rajasthan	50.13	36.59	48.60
Tamil Nadu	26.33	20.99	24.91
Uttar Pradesh	52.31	41.72	50.91
West Bengal	38.50	21.61	35.17
All India	42.18	29.29	40.14

Source: Government of India, Ministry of Home Affairs, Sample Registration System, New Delhi, 1988.

TABLE 4. PERCENTAGE DISTRIBUTION OF DEATHS BY MAJOR CAUSE IN INDIA (RURAL)

Major Cause Groups	1988	1989	1990	1991	1992
Senility	24.7	23.8	24.4	23.8	23.5
Coughs	20.3	20.2	18.8	18.9	19.6
Diseases of Circulatory System	10.00	10.9	11.1	11.1	10.8
Causes Peculiar to Infancy	9.8	9.8	9.8	10.2	9.6
Accidents and Injuries	6.5	7.4	8.5	8.5	8.7
Other Clear Symptoms	8.8	8.2	8.5	8.3	8.4
Fevers	8.0	7.4	7.3	7.3	7.7
Digestive Disorders	6.5	6.6	6.2	6.4	6.2
Central Nervous System Disorders	4.6	4.8	4.3	4.4	4.5
Child Birth and Pregnancy	0.8	0.9	1.0	1.1	1.0
All Causes	100	100	100	100.0	100.0

Source: Government of India, Ministry of Home Affairs, Survey of Causes of Death (Rural) India, 1992, New Delhi, 1994.

TABLE 5. NOTIFIED CASES OF CHOLERA, MALARIA, KALA AZAR
AND JAPANESE ENCEPHALITIS, 1986-91

Year	Cholera C	Cholera D	Malaria C	Malaria D	Kala Azar C	Kala Azar D	J.E. C	J.E. D
1986	4,211	71	17,92,167	323	14,079*	47	-	-
1987	11,423	224	16,63,284	188	19,179*	77	9,080	1,596
1988	8,957	215	18,54,830	209	22,739	131	16,384	3,304
1989	5,044	72	20,17,823	268	34,489	497	22,263	3,511
1990	3,704	87	20,18,783	353	57,742	606	16,757	2,984
1991	7,088	150	21,20,472	421	61,438	869	11,995	2,290

Note: *Figures for Bihar alone.
C = cases notified; D = fatalities
Source: Government of India, CBHI, Health Information of India, 1991, New Delhi, 1992.

TABLE 6. PERCENTAGE DISTRIBUTION OF HOUSEHOLDS ACCORDING TO
PROTEIN ENERGY ADEQUACY STATUS

State	1975-9 P+	1975-9 E+	1988-90 P+	1988-90 E+
Kerala	69.7	39.0	71.5	39.7
Tamil Nadu	83.0	54.8	62.1	32.1
Karnataka	96.7	82.1	91.4	62.1
Andhra Pradesh	88.5	67.1	82.6	58.5
Maharashtra	90.2	56.5	88.0	49.5
Gujarat	92.8	50.3	92.8	52.7
Madhya Pradesh	97.0	55.1	96.0	78.4
Pooled	88.2	58.0	83.5	53.3

Note: P+ = Protein Adequate.
E+ = Energy Adequate.
Source: National Institute of Nutrition, National Nutrition Monitoring Bureau, *Report of Repeat Surveys (1988-90)*, Hyderabad, 1991.

The pooled data for the seven states for which the data on protein and energy adequacy of households is available, indicates a decline in the proportion of households able to meet their energy and protein needs. This is particularly marked in states such as Tamil Nadu, Andhra Pradesh, Karnataka and Maharashtra.

Table 7 presents the data on the energy intake of pre-school children.

While the proportion of pre-school children with severe undernutrition has declined, there has been an increase in the proportion of

TABLE 7. ENERGY INTAKE OF PRE-SCHOOL CHILDREN BY NUTRITIONAL STATUS

Nutritional Status Weight for Age	Energy Intake of Children			
	1975-9	1988-90	% of 1975-9	1988-90
More than 90	1035	1013	3.6	4.6
90-75: Mild	995	988	29.3	33.6
75-60: Moderate	884	928	52.7	52.4
Less than 60: Severe	812	796	14.4	9.4

Source: Same as Table 6.

children exhibiting mild under-nutrition. What is disquieting is that there have been declines in energy consumption among all groups of children with the exception of those moderately under-nourished.

The data above are evidence that the state of health sector development in the country has been dismal indeed. We have had many 'quick track' initiatives in the past which have simply failed to deliver. Perhaps it is time to recognize that building an epidemiologically relevant public health system is a long-drawn process allowing no quick technological options but dependent instead on a universally accessible, comprehensive system of primary health care interlinked with a pattern of overall development where the needs of the majority of the population are not ignored.

REFERENCES

Banerji, D., 1971. 'Tuberculosis as a Problem of Social Planning in India', *NIHAE Bulletin* 4(1).

Basu, R.N., Z. Jezek and N.A. Ward, 1979. *The Eradication of Smallpox from India*, WHO, New Delhi.

Cassen, R.H., 1978. *India: Population, Economy, Society*, Macmillan, Hong Kong.

Government of India, 1946. *Report of the Health Survey and Development Committee*, Government of India Press, New Delhi.

————, 1952. *First Five Year Plan*, Planning Commission, New Delhi.

————, 1961. *Report of the Health Survey and Planning Committee*, Ministry of Health, New Delhi.

————, 1963. *Report of the Special Committee on the Preparation for the Entry of the National Malaria Eradicaion Programme into the Maintenance Phase*, Ministry of Health, New Delhi.

————, 1966a. *Report of the Committee on Basic Health Services* (Mukherji Committee), Ministry of Health and Family Planning, New Delhi.

————, 1966b. *Report of the Special Committee Appointed to Review Staffing Pattern and Financial Position under the Family Planning Programme*, Ministry of Health and Family Planning, New Delhi.

————, 1969-74. *Fourth Five Year Plan 1969-74*, Planning Commission, New Delhi.

————, 1973. *Report of the Committee on Multi-Purpose Workers Under Health and Family Planning Programme*, Ministry of Health and Family Planning, New Delhi.

————, 1975. *Health Services and Medical Education: A Programme for Immediate Action: Report of the Group on Medical Education and Support Manpower*, Ministry of Health and Family Planning, New Delhi.

————, 1978. *Report of the Shah Commission of Enquiry*, vol. III, Ministry of Home Affairs, New Delhi.

————, 1980. *Report of the Working Group on Population Policy*, Planning Commission, New Delhi.

————, 1982. *Statement on National Health Policy*, Ministry of Health and Family Welfare, New Delhi.

————, 1986. *National Population Policy*, Ministry of Health and Family Welfare, New Delhi.

————, 1993. *India Country Scenario: An Update*, Ministry of Health and Family Welfare, National AIDS Control Programme, New Delhi.

————, 1994. *Draft National Population Policy*, Ministry of Health and Family Welfare, New Delhi.

Grodos, D. and X. de Bethune, 1988. 'Les Interventions Sanitaires Selectives: Un Piege Pour Les Politiques De Sante Tiers Monde', English Abstract: W. Bichmann, *Social Science and Medicine* 26(9).

Hodgson, D., 1988. 'Orthodoxy and Revisionism in American Demography', *Population and Development Review* XIV(4).

Indian Council of Social Science Research and Indian Council of Medical Research, 1981. *Health For All: An Alternative Strategy—Report of a Study Group Set Up Jointly by ICSSR and ICMR*, Indian Institute of Education, Pune, 1981.

Newell, K.W., 1978. 'Selective Primary Health Care: The Counter Revolution', *Social Science and Medicine*, 26(9).

Qadeer, I., 1994. 'The World Development Report 1993: The Brave New World of Primary Health Care', *Social Scientist* 22(912).

Smith, D.L., and J.H. Bryant, 1988. 'Building the Infrastructure for Primary Health Care: An Overview of Vertical and Integrated Approaches', *Social Science and Medicine* 26(9).

UN Advisory Mission, 1966. *Report of the Family Planning Programme in India*, New York.

World Bank, 1995. *India's Family Welfare Programme: Toward a Reproductive and Child Health Approach*, Population and Human Resources Operations Division, New Delhi.

# Seminar Proceedings*

INTRODUCTION

The National Seminar on 'Gender, Health and Reproduction', held at the India International Centre, New Delhi on 16-17 November 1995, brought together professionals in the field of health and NGO stalwarts who had undertaken bold initiatives in this field. As Swapna Mukhopadhyay, Director, ISST put it, the seminar enabled the participants to share the rich experience of listening to both the thinkers and the doers. In this process, the whole canvas of India's health programmes since independence came in for scrutiny, in an atmosphere of lively debate.

The seminar was hosted by the Institute of Social Studies Trust (ISST), New Delhi as one of its activities under the on-going project on 'Poverty, Gender Inequality and Reproductive Choice' sponsored by the MacArthur Foundation.

THE PROGRAMME

The opening session of the seminar focused on the 'Macro Scenario on Health and Well Being' with special reference to women's health. There were presentations by Krishna Soman of ISST, New Delhi; Ravi Duggal of CEHAT (Centre for Enquiry into Health and Allied Themes), Bombay; and A.K. Shiva Kumar, UNICEF. The session was chaired by N.H. Antia of FRCH (the Foundation for Research in Community Health) and the expert commentator was Leela Visaria.

The second session consisted of two presentations by ISST, New Delhi, based on their findings from research projects on reproductive choice. This session was chaired by Mohan Rao and Saraswathy Ganapathy provided expert comments.

The morning session of the second day was devoted to presentations made by three NGOs working at the grassroots level in the field of health. The first presentation was made jointly by N.H. Antia and Nerges Mistry of FRCH, Bombay, followed by T.K. Sundari Ravindran of RUWSEC (Rural Women's Social Education Centre), Tamil Nadu and

*The draft Seminar Proceedings was prepared by Claire Noronha, Consultant, ISST.

S.N. Chaudhuri of CINI (Child In Need Institute), Calcutta. The session was chaired by K.S. Krishnaswamy and the expert comments were given by D. Banerji and Subhash Mendhapurkar, Director, SUTRA (Society for Uplift through Rural Action), Himachal Pradesh.

The final session focused on policy issues and new research agenda in which Mohan Rao gave an elaborate description of India's health policies since independence. The session was chaired by Shanti Ghosh for which K.S. Krishnaswamy was the expert commentator.

PRESENTATIONS AND DISCUSSIONS

Session 1

Paper 1. Planning for the Health of Women: The Indian Experience—Krishna Soman, ISST, New Delhi

Paper 2. Health Sector Financing in the Context of Women's Health—Ravi Duggal, CEHAT, Bombay.

Paper 3. Equality and Political Participation: Their Significance for Women's Well-Being— A.K.Shiva Kumar, UNICEF, New Delhi.

Krishna Soman's paper, which was a part of an ISST research project titled 'Poverty, Gender Inequality and Reproductive Choice', set the right tone for the seminar by drawing a retrospective on planning for the health of women since independence.

According to Soman, our planners had always perceived women's health in the context of motherhood. The Bhore (1946) and Sokhey (1948) Committees recommended maternal and child health as a priority issue in the first five years because of the disturbingly high maternal mortality rate of 12.9 per 1,000 live births at the time of independence.

The two committees viewed health as a responsibility of the State and recommended a minimum budget of not less than 10 per cent of the total annual budget outlay for this sector. But right through the plans, the investment in health has averaged only about 3 per cent of the outlay. There was also a demand on manpower and resources by other vertical programmes, most especially, the programme to limit population growth. Despite slogans like 'Development is the Best Contraceptive', population control remains a pressure on all health programmes. This shift in policy has further weakened the programmes and infrastructure.

After almost five decades of health interventions, there has been some improvement in the maternal mortality rate (1.9 per 1000 live births) possibly owing to more aseptic conditions of delivery, but the percentage of maternal deaths from anaemia has shown only marginal decrease from 23.3 per cent in 1936 to 19.1 per cent in 1985-90. This reveals 'that the general "ill health" of women leading to maternal death has remained almost stagnant' in spite of the MCH and the Anaemia Prophylaxis Programme. This points to the fact that 'we must understand women's health in its totality'. The declining sex ratio is part of this sorry state of affairs. Soman cautioned that if the infrastructure remains ineffective and inadequate, the present call for reproductive health programmes will meet the same fate as the MCH programme.

Ravi Duggal outlined a system which could provide vastly improved health services. He expressed the view that although 'the health system views women in terms of their uterus', this has failed to provide women with safe pregnancy, maternity or contraceptive benefits. The MMR and the percentage of unsafe births is very high in rural areas.

Duggal showed that the utilization of maternal and child health services is poor across classes in both rural as well as urban areas. He disagreed totally with the idea of treating reproductive health as a special programme for he thinks, this would, like the MCH programme, make women mere targets for population control.

According to Duggal, the failure of programmes was also caused by mismatch of Centre-state priorities as health is a state subject while health policy and planning is done at the Centre. He asserted that the government should create a single system which assures universal coverage with equity. Emphasizing the need for redefining primary health care in terms of people's need, he further stressed the need for the states to allocate at least 5 per cent of the GDP for health services and devise a system common for people in rural as well as urban areas. To overcome the shortage of personnel and equipment, he suggested the utilization of the private sector with a system such as a fixed capitation fee per family.

Duggal felt that with proper planning and management, the virtues of the private sector which make it so attractive (its convenience, personalized care and efficiency) could be replicated by the public sector. The system had to be accountable to the local community. Private facilities also had to be monitored, standardized and relocated if necessary. He opined that this necessitated a fivefold increase in finance which could be raised from existing resources, from employers in the organized sector and by special incentives. He advised against direct payment for health needs and stated that much improvement was possible even within the existing system if states played a greater role in health planning.

After the presentation by Duggal for a better health system came a reminder from the UN that India was really at the bottom of the league as far as gender bias was concerned.

A.K. Shiva Kumar, in his paper, ranked India on a world scale as per the UN's latest yardstick—the GDI or Gender Development Index as per UNDP's Human Development Report (1995). The GDI was simply the HDI (Human Development Index) adjusted for gender inequality. He stated that India ranked 99th out of 130 countries for which the GDI had been calculated, and given the anti-female biases in our society, this revelation was not surprising.

Kumar also calculated the GDI for different states as per the methodology used in the Human Development Report (1995), and discovered the startling interstate disparities with Kerala (0.540) having the highest GDI and ranking 74th on the scale and Uttar Pradesh (0.308) ranking 116th. Only fourteen countries in the world have a lower GDI than Uttar Pradesh.

He pointed out that it was difficult to correlate gender inequality with women's health, as the information base on women's health is very poor. As several studies reveal, women's ill-health is also grossly under-reported and often scarcely even perceived. This is compounded by a strong male bias in the use of hospitals even in urban areas.

The lack of services like health and education also affects women's health. He cited the example of Kerala where 90 per cent of all deliveries are done with qualified medical assistance while as in Bihar, Orissa, Uttar Pradesh and Rajasthan, considered poor health states, 80 per cent of women do not receive medical assistance.

According to Shiva Kumar, a high income level is not essential for good health as China, Cuba and Sri Lanka have shown. Punjab has twice Kerala's per capita income, but its infant mortality rate (IMR) is four times that of Kerala. In his opinion, the situation can change even in the poorer states, given the political will and the right inputs.

He further correlated women's health in India with greater freedom. He cited the example of Kerala and Manipur, two good-health states, where women enjoy greater freedom in marital and occupational choice. Even if one looked at active political participation by comparing female voter turnout in Kerala and Manipur with that in the 'poor health states', Kerala and Manipur show a significantly higher degree of political participation, he added.

SESSION 1: DISCUSSION

The discussant, Leela Visaria, felt it was a good time to debate about the issue of another reproductive-health-based vertical programme for women. She felt that reproductive health *per se* had not been addressed so far except for a brief mention of ante-natal care and family planning.

She expressed the need for reproductive health care services to take off widely as 92 per cent of women suffer from gynaecological problems. The Bhore Committee had recommended a gynaecological care ratio of 1:20,000 which at present stands at a low 1:50,000.

The ensuing discussion focused on the following issues:

The issue of choosing between a vertically designed reproductive health programme versus designing reproductive health issues within a comprehensive health package. Several speakers supported Ravi Duggal's argument that a vertically designed reproductive health care may turn out to be yet another programme aimed at the control of the uterus. N.H. Antia even felt vertical programmes were themselves a costly inheritance from the West where everything is compartmentalized. Shanti Ghosh disputed this and felt that a majority of Indian demographers prefer an integrated reproductive-cum-mother-and-child health care package. This would also take care of children who at present are abandoned after immunization.

On financing the health system. The speakers agreed that the health budget was inadequate and had declined further after liberalization. And given the present scenario it was unlikely to go up. Shanti Ghosh felt that a small fee for public services was unlikely to be grudged. A referral system was very necessary. She added that 80 per cent of the cases brought to the hospital could be handled by the local doctors. N.H. Antia expressed the opinion that good health care is cheap, while bad health care is expensive.

On the positive role of education. N.H. Antia was of the opinion that spending on education would give better health than spending on medical services. Subhash Mendhapurkar disagreed by expressing the view that formal education in Himachal Pradesh had disempowered women and caused the death of local traditions in health care.

In this context, Swapna Mukhopadhyay (ISST), mentioned that data from the Uttar Pradesh survey currently being analysed at ISST suggest that the links between formal school education of women and contraceptive use is very tenuous, while some variables reflecting higher awareness like exposure to radio, appear to have greater correlation with the latter.

On the traditional knowledge base. Several speakers felt that traditional knowledge was a valuable resource which had to be studied and integrated where useful. 'Don't be excessively sentimental', said Ghosh. She had seen the horrors of scarring and maiming by the ill-advised use of traditional methods.

On the role of political participation of women. While Antia felt that it was a good parameter for development, Subhash Mendhapurkar referred to the recently held panchayat elections in Himachal Pradesh where 80 per cent of the women reported that the papers were snatched from them as soon as they entered the booths.

SESSION 2

Paper 4. Poverty, Gender Inequality and Reproduction: Some Findings from a Household Survey in Uttar Pradesh—Swapna Mukhopadhyay, Praachi Tewari Gandhi and R. Savithri, ISST, New Delhi.

Paper 5. The Contours of Reproductive Choice for Women: Findings from a Micro Survey—Swapna Mukhopadhyay and Surekha Garimella, ISST, New Delhi.

These papers were based on preliminary investigations into data sets from two household surveys. They intended to map the overlap between gender inequality and reproductive choice with the long-term objective of evolving a more gender-sensitive population policy.

The analysis in Paper 4 concentrated on assessing the impact of poverty and gender inequality on reproductive choice as research on demographic change had identified variables which acted as explanatory variables in reproductive choice. The study was conducted both in Karnataka and Uttar Pradesh but at the time of writing this paper only the Uttar Pradesh data set was available. Hence, the paper has considered only the Uttar Pradesh sample. The total sample size was 1,078 households spread over 35 villages. About 798 women in the reproductive age group (15-49 years) were interviewed and of these, husbands of

529 women were also interviewed. A large percentage of those surveyed lived below the poverty line and were mostly illiterate.

The papers primarily investigate the effect of poverty on reproductive health and reproductive choice among women in selected rural areas. Poverty affects not only access to goods and services but also health, at the curative and preventive levels. The poor health status of women affects reproductive choice in much the same way as infant mortality does and both have been shown to work against family planning.

The effect of gender discrimination on reproductive choice is not well researched in India, although several studies have suggested a link between reproductive choice and the education of women, their participation in the work force, their decision-making authority within the family and their physical and economic autonomy. However, the complexity of the pattern of interlinkages often makes it difficult to predict the direction of linkages between binary variables. The analysis also tested existing hypotheses on fertility patterns and contraceptive use.

Summary of Paper 4

Bivariate analysis: some results. Current contraceptive use was cross-tabulated with several variables, many of which have been used in multiple regressions.

Correlation of contraceptive use with
  (a) Religion or caste—not significant.
  (b) Age at marriage—positive for both males and females.
  (c) Level of education of men (women were largely illiterate)—extent of contraceptive use was found higher for all levels of education but almost double where men were graduates.
  (d) Women earning independently—since the number was very small, the correlation was not clear.
  (e) Women's control over household income—not positive except where women also earn independently.
  (f) Women's decision-making authority regarding her work outside the home, family size, children's schooling—no correlation.
  (g) Desire to have more sons both among males and females—absence of family planning.
  (h) Poverty—positive correlation with rise in per capita income (PCI).

Differences in male and female perceptions. Women seem to have imbibed gender-discriminatory values. Wives say they would depend on sons and not daughters in old age, and that they would educate sons more than their daughters. Husbands were less discriminatory, at least in their pronouncements.

Women feel they have some autonomy in decisions about their work, the size of the family and the children's schooling. The men did not seem to agree with their claim. About contraceptive use there was a 20 per cent contradiction. Husbands' claims about using condom or having been sterilized were often not corroborated by their wives. Most couples intended placing the burden of contraception on the women.

Multivariate analysis: some results. A number of multiple regressions were run with fertility as the dependent variable.

Female literacy has repeatedly come up with insignificant t-values as compared to female exposure to radio which appears to have greater explanatory power. Poverty, as measured by per capita income (PCI), appears to have insignificant explanatory powers determining fertility. However, when a quadratic term was introduced, results improved considerably. In other words, fertility appears to be strongly correlated with per capita income in a parabolic manner, with high fertility being associated with very high and very low levels of income.

Paper 5 was a report on an ISST research project which arose from the perception that reproductive choice went much beyond contraception alternatives. It touched the self-esteem and autonomy of women. Information in the survey was sought among other things on the negotiation of sexual relations within marriage, sexual subordination and the material conditions which influenced choice.

In Phase I of the project, there were group discussions about reproductive health needs and rights, etc. The women were less concerned, it was found, with reproductive issues *per se* as compared to issues of employment, poverty, sanitation, health services, etc. This echoes one of the major concerns brought up by the current population control/development debate.

In Phase II of the project, information was collected through a structured questionnaire remarkable for the delicacy of the information it sought to elicit.

About 200 women in the reproductive age group were surveyed in four locations across the country with the help of local NGO working in the district. For 50 couples in each sample, the male member was also included in the survey. For this report, data from two locations, Kumaon and Delhi, were presented. Some of the salient features of the sample were as follows:

Pregnancy profile. The average age at marriage was between 14-19 years. The average number of pregnancies was 3.94 and 3.12 in the Delhi and Kumaon samples respectively. Some proportion of the women (22-30 per cent) had received ante-natal care, but the majority had their deliveries at home.

Reproductive health profile. A larger proportion of Kumaoni women reported health problems ranging from menstrual disorders to giddiness, etc. When medical help was sought, it was mostly private, and availed of largely by the Delhi women who, however, expressed dissatisfaction with its effectiveness.

Views on contraception. Awareness of the usefulness and the methods of contraception was high especially in the Delhi sample but in both cases, more than two-thirds did not use any method at all. Women expressed tubectomy as the preferred method of contraception as it involves fewer complications and is a permanent method of birth control. A fairly high incidence of complications connected with various contraceptive methods was reported.

Sexual relations and unwanted pregnancies. On the question of coercive marital sex, women generally claimed they could refuse and did do so on occasions but more than 60 per cent also said they faced abuse and violence, both physical and verbal, if they did so. Very few admit to 'unwanted pregnancy' and that too only if they had many children. Two-thirds have tried abortion if the pregnancy was unwanted.

Abortion. Women were unwilling to talk about personal experience of abortion but could talk of that of other women, and many felt that it was immoral. Equal percentages opted to have an abortion and to continue with the pregnancy, if it was unwanted. While in Delhi women used government facilities, in Kumaon, women resorted to home remedies.

Gender roles. In general, men were ignorant and insensitive about the health problems of their wives. There was a lack of awareness even about the number of pregnancies, miscarriages and abortions experienced by their wives. Men generally felt they have a tougher life than that of women, even if both husband and wife work outside the house. They also report health problems more frequently than women do. Feeling strongly against termination of any pregnancy, they also had fixed beliefs about gender roles.

SESSION 2: DISCUSSION

Much of the discussion centred around research methodology in social sciences, such as length of survey questionnaries and nature of questions probed.

The discussant, Saraswathi Ganapathy, expressed the view that one needed to be cautious about defining complex issues like 'autonomy' and even 'ante-natal care'. She also felt that sensitive questions needed very sensitive interviewers and more so in an immensely heterogeneous society like ours. She questioned the nature and methodology of very large-scale surveys.

D.V. Rukmini felt that questionnaire surveys were useful and, as an example, pointed out how the data showed the media was better at generating awareness than just education. She felt that a few more variables could be used for the regressions. Mukhopadhyay welcomed the suggestions which were made about further investigation into the data sets and assured that the suggestions would be incorporated in subsequent analysis of the data.

SESSION 3

Paper 6. Women in Panchayati Raj: Implications of 'Health for All'— N.H. Antia and Nerges Mistry, FRCH, Bombay.
Paper 7. Reproductive Health: An NGO Initiative in Chengalpattu, Tamil Nadu—T. K. Sundari Ravindran.
Paper 8. Women's Health in the Evolution of CINI—S.N. Chaudhuri.

In the current scenario of cynicism about developments in the area of health in India, the three speakers, N.H. Antia, Sundari Ravindran and S.N. Chaudhuri sounded refreshingly positive about 'Health for All'. All of them are working through local communities to initiate health activities.

N.H. Antia, with the impatience of a man who had tried the conventional methods and found them wanting, exploded several myths about health.

Myth 1: health belongs to the medical profession. He stated that health had been appropriated by the medical profession who were taught only about the failure of health. According to him, health must be handed back to people. The medical profession is only the last 'pillar of health' as the J.P. Nayak Committee had pointed out. The other pillars are nutrition, employment, education, particularly female education, water, housing and sanitation.

Myth 2: health care is expensive. About 80 per cent of our illnesses are those associated with malnutrition and communicable diseases.

Antia expressed the view that it is the western science which has made medical care expensive. In India, with her strong traditional remedies, most diseases can be tackled at the local level and at low expenditure. He also added that only 10 per cent of illnesses require high expense.

According to Antia, Rs 100 per capita expenditure is enough to give an efficient system. The Indian Council of Medical Research Report (ICMR) (1980) has stated that 90 per cent of health care is best done at the local (100,000 people) level.

Antia felt that panchayati raj could give power to the people and that through it, people could exercise control over their own health needs.

N. Mistry then outlined the 'Parinche' project of FRCH under which ordinary village women are trained to undertake programmes on health care. This project, which is going on in some rural areas of Pune district is being handled by Antia and herself and is a systematic exploration of the role which village women can play given the potential of panchayati raj. The project, of which health is one component also provides training in areas of watershed management, rural banking, library and veterinary services.

T.S. Ravindran then spoke of the evolution of RUWSEC (Rural Women's Social Centre, Chengalpattu), a grass-roots women's organization promoting women's empowerment which evolved from an adult education programme in a village in Tamil Nadu. The women, who were dalits, and working as adult educators, began to question their oppression as poor dalit women. Most of them were employed as agricultural labourers who began to challenge the class, caste and gender subordination which compromised women's well-being and health status as health services remained inaccessible to them.

The main strategy was to organize women into *sanghams* or associations through which they could discuss their problems and demand their rights. Today the organization boasts of various activities which include:

— community-based action for health promotion through a community health worker;

- publication and distribution of popular educational material on health;
- educational and empowerment programmes for adolescents;
- programmes for men on reproductive health issues.

The movement is showing perceptible change in the local community. Nearly all hamlets have initiated action for protected water supply. Immunization programme has covered 80 per cent of children and fewer get diarrhoea. 'Hospital deliveries' have gone up from 25 per cent to about 49 per cent between 1989 and 1991. As a result of women's empowerment, many of the women have stood up against medical inaction and inefficiency.

Discussing the limitations of the organization, Ravindran added that the organization has remained low profile and not been able to influence policy in a significant way and secondly, it is dependent on external finance.

The major achievement of the organization is that it has 'tapped and nurtured local women's leadership to take charge of an organization and develop it imaginatively'.

Samir Chaudhuri discussed the evolution of the Child In Need Institute (CINI) which began in a village on the outskirts of Calcutta city in 1974. It aimed at tackling morbidity and mortality among children under the age of five. The health workers who were locally recruited, were provided training. Literacy and income generation programmes became important components from 1980 onwards especially after the formation of *mahila mandals* in CINI areas.

Since women were very vocal about the lack of medical facilities in their areas, health care services beginning with ante-natal services came to be provided, for which the village *dais* were given an orientation training. As the socio-economic conditions and the health of children improved, there was a demand for family planning and welfare services. Similarly, health services were provided to commercial sex workers when the problems related to STD (Sexually Transmitted Diseases) became rampant in certain pockets of the city.

Gradually, the approach changed from a clinic-based approach to a community-based integrated services approach which includes the education of the girl child. CINI endeavours to provide comprehensive care for women and children though many gaps still exist in this ambitious plan.

SESSION 3: DISCUSSION

The discussant, D. Banerji, remarked that the public health system had failed, but even the NGO movement had been coopted by the power elite, the government and the multinational companies.

Several important issues which were brought forth are:

— NGOs are not necessarily gender-sensitive.
— Next to dowry, the cause of rural indebtedness is sickness.
— At the danger of being simplistic, most NGOs tend to be naive about the political process and treat panchayati raj as a magic wand. They oversimplify complex problems of health. Health problems cannot be reduced to health financing.

Animated discussion followed on many issues.

One speaker felt that the issue of reproductive health needs to be placed within the life situation of women. Also, NGOs were too simplistic about reproductive health and often neglected the pre-menstrual and post-menopausal stages.

Shanti Ghosh felt that it is important not to neglect the MCH programme as maternal deaths are still a major problem in India.

In answer to the query about the relationship between the NGOs and the public health system, S. Ravindran mentioned that her NGO cooperated with the public health system for providing immunization and ante-natal health care. Before RUWSEC became active, the ANMs did not bother about the dalit section but now its existence is recognized. For gynaecological problems and STD, since the PHC did not provide help, RUWSEC undertakes this work. About the panchayati raj it was felt that since the system was still evolving, it was important for people to gain access to the right information for awareness.

S. Mukhopadhyay brought up an interesting and tricky issue of how one could ensure that the rural community and the system was not corrupted by the consumerist culture. Antia agreed with the potential danger but stated that at present the major preoccupation in rural areas is only relief from pain.

Summing up the main issues and insights thrown up by the three speakers and the ensuing discussion, Krishnaswamy noted the following:

— The question of 'Health for All' goes beyond mere provision of health services.

- The basic problems at the ground level are communicable diseases, which can be tackled by the people themselves with adequate support and information and at fairly low levels of expenditure.
- Poverty alleviation programmes are necessary or there is no escape from malnutrition and its consequences.
- Oversimplifying the issues should be avoided.
- Empowerment of women is possible through *sanghams*, *mandals*, etc. It is possible to give knowledge through simple training methods.
- The panchayati raj gives opportunity but has its limitations of money and power. Panchayati raj institutions also are dominated by vested interests.

SESSION 4

Paper 9. India's Augean Stables: The Unfinished Health Agenda—Mohan Rao

Mohan Rao, in a panoramic survey of the fifty years after independence, threw light on our lack of progress in the field of health and the main reasons for this. He referred to the Bhore Committee which had laid down the guiding principle, whereby provision of health services was the responsibility of the State, and was to be available irrespective of the ability to pay.

The First Plan emphasized preventive services but importance was given to technological solutions. Rao mentioned that India was the first country to launch a family planning programme apart from other vertical programmes for the control of malaria, smallpox, etc. Even the international agencies were greatly in favour of these programmes.

He further added that during the First and the Second Plan periods, the health sector obtained 3.3 and 3 per cent of the total outlays respectively, of which 60 per cent was allocated to curative health services and medical education. Public health remained low on priority. As a consequence of this approach, while hospitals and medical colleges came up, PHCs did not.

In the Third Plan, recommendations were made to upgrade the existing health infrastructure including PHCs. Efforts were made to launch the National Small Pox Eradication Programme (NSEP) and National Tuberculosis Programme (NTP). Elaborating on the programmes drafted in the five-year plans, Rao further added that during the Fourth Plan, the budget for health shrank and that for family planning rose, drastically.

A developmentalist perspective was adopted in the Fifth Plan with the objective of providing minimum health facilities and nutrition and this was integrated with family planning. With the declaration of emergency a host of anti-natalist measures were announced to control the population due to which the family planning programmes suffered a major setback.

In spite of a call for de-professionalization of health care (Shrivastava Committee) and the Alma Ata pledge of Health for All in 1978, the Sixth Plan continued to emphasize vertical programmes and family planning. The Seventh Plan took note of the poor health infrastructure in rural areas but wanted to grapple with major non-communicable health problems like cancer and heart disease.

The Eighth Plan document admitted the failure to control communicable diseases and population growth. It found the shortfall in PHCs 'staggering' and the resources required 'astronomical'. It is now relying on private initiative and reviewing the concept of free medical care. Under structural adjustment, central government expenditure on health has declined still further and continues to decline. All is not well with the family planning programme either. Rao felt that the attempt to push hormonal contraceptives is a feeble attempt to give a new lease of life to the family planning programme.

SESSION 4: DISCUSSION

The discussant, K.S. Krishnaswamy, remarked that there was a general agreement that health policy had been no policy at all but a mixture of short-term approaches undertaken with specific objectives. These objectives were motivated by political pressures both from within the country and from international bodies.

DIRECTIONS FOR THE FUTURE

Krishnaswamy made the following suggestions for research in order to formulate a new health policy.

— Needs and priorities need to be clearly specified. Several areas have to be reformulated to ensure a sustainable policy of Health for All. These include the prevention of epidemics as well as morbidity.
— Institutional patterns best suited to the needs and priorities need to be developed.

- Technological patterns best suited to our needs require to be nurtured.
- On the issue of payment, he said there were two distinct schools of thought which need discussion: (a) Health facilities should remain free of cost; (b) Health facilities should be available on payment.

This reverses the basics of the Bhore Committee. The private sector was there to meet health needs and those unable to pay could be subsidized on a rational basis.

The World Bank (1993) has recommended privatization of health services and increasing productivity but for basic health services an increased role of the public sector is necessary. The central government cannot be the agency for this.

- *Eradication of epidemics.* This needs to be taken care of through development and changes in infrastructure policy. It requires investment, to ensure that epidemics do not become endemic, and also to ensure proper nutrition of women, especially those in the reproductive age group, and of growing children.
- *The prevention of morbidity.* The strategy should be participatory and follow an integrated approach to community health and should include employment generation.

What Can Be Done at Present

Krishnaswamy also made some suggestions about what we could do at present considering that the government with its short-sighted approach would not make more funds available. His suggestions included the following:

- Train a large number of primary health workers and reduce the proliferation of the bureaucracy in the name of health services.
- Carefully reorganize reproductive health care both from the health and the bureaucratic points of view, and see that the system is implemented.
- Pay more attention to preventive health care, especially towards water borne diseases, STDs, TB, and malaria.
- Improve nutrition of children with careful examination of schemes like the ICDS.
- Carefully monitor private health services for quality of care and nature of charges.

The concluding discussion focused on several issues raised by Rao and Krishnaswamy:

(a) *Public health services.* It was pointed out that though investments are made, quality of service is absent. As far as the staff is concerned, not even 50 per cent of the doctors are in position. It was felt that the staff in public hospitals could be put on rotation.

(b) *Cost recovery for health care.* Opinion was in favour of a universal health scheme, which can be insurance linked.

Mohan Rao pointed out that the Canadian government had discontinued health fees as they found out that it affected the health-seeking behaviour of the disadvantaged. Costly services like dialysis only were available on payment.

(c) *Use of traditional wisdom*: All those with experience seemed to agree that *vaids*, homeopaths, etc., felt a lack of status and expertise and wished to receive training in the allopathic system of medicine. Mohan Rao reported that research had shown traditional systems which had decayed after the sixth century, received a fillip during the Muslim rule and then decayed again.

(d) *Poverty, malnutrition and health.* It was pointed out that deprivation has a direct impact on health. Women have to travel long distances in search of water and fuel and due to lack of amenities, their health always takes a backseat. This is compounded by a high rate of illiteracy among women. In case of infants, malnutrition is rampant from six months to two years because of the sheer lack of knowledge of what the child needs. The problem is carried forward into the next few years and the child gets 60 per cent of what he needs even at the age of three, four and five.

At the end of the concluding session, Swapna Mukhopadhayay thanked all the speakers and the participants for their contribution and meaningful interaction. She added that the seminar had been a valuable experience for all at ISST.

Seminar Agenda

THURSDAY, 16.11.95

9.30-10.00 a.m. Welcome address: *Dr Swapna Mukhopadhyay*, Director, ISST

10.00-1.00 P.M. SESSION I

MACRO SCENARIO ON HEALTH AND WELL-BEING WITH SPECIAL REFERENCE TO REPRODUCTIVE HEALTH

Chairperson: Dr N.H. Antia
Expert Commentator: Dr Leela Visaria

Presentations:

1. Planning for Health of Women: The Indian experience
   Ms Krishna Soman
2. Health Sector Financing in the Context of Women's Health
   Dr Ravi Duggal
3. Gender Equality and Political Participation Implications for Good Health
   Dr A.K. Shiva Kumar

11.15-11.30 a.m. Tea/Coffee
Comments and Discussions
1.00-2.00 p.m. Lunch Break

2.00-5.00 P.M. SESSION II

MICRO STUDIES ON GENDER AND REPRODUCTION

Chairperson: Dr Ravi Duggal
Expert Commentator: Dr Saraswathy Ganapathy
Ms. D.V. Rukmini

Presentations:

1. Poverty, Gender Inequality and Reproductive Choice: Some Findings from a Household Survey in U.P.-ISST
2. The Contours of Reproductive Choice for Poor Women: Findings from a Micro Survey-ISST

3.15-3.30 p.m. Tea/Coffee
Comments and Discussions

FRIDAY, 17.11.95

10.00 - 1.00 P.M.   SESSION III

NGO INITIATIVES IN THE FIELD OF HEALTH CARE

Chairperson: Dr K.S. Krishnaswamy
Expert Commentator: Prof. D. Banerji
　　　　　　　　　　　Mr Subhash Mendhapurkar

Presentations:

1. Women in Panchayati Raj: Implications for 'Health for All'
   Dr N.H. Antia and Dr Nerges Mistry
2. Reaching Women Through Children at CINI
   Dr S.N. Chaudhuri
3. Rural Women's Social Education Centre, Chengalpattu: Case study of Grassroots Organization Working for the Health Promotion Through Women's Empowerment
   Dr T.K. Sundari Ravindran

11.30 a.m. Tea/Coffee
Comments and Discussions

2.00-4.30 P.M.   SESSION IV

POLICY ISSUES AND NEW RESEARCH AGENDA

Chairperson: Dr Shanti Ghosh
Expert Commentator: Dr K.S. Krishnaswamy

Presentations:

　　India's Augean Stables: The Unfinished Health Agenda
　　Dr Mohan Rao

3.30 p.m. Tea/Coffee
Comments and Discussions

LIST OF PARTICIPANTS

1. Dr N.H. Antia
   Director
   Foundation for Research in
   Community Health (FRCH)
   Mumbai
2. Dr S.N. Chaudhuri
   Director
   Child in Need Institute (CINI)
   Calcutta
3. Dr T.K. Sundari Ravindran
   F-17, Haus Khas Enclave
   New Delhi
4. Dr Mohan Rao
   Asst. Professor
   School of Social Sciences, JNU
   New Delhi
5. Dr A.K. Shiva Kumar
   Consultant, UNICEF
   New Delhi
6. Dr Ravi Duggal
   Consultant
   Centre for Enquiry into Health
   and Allied Themes (CEHAT)
   Mumbai
7. Dr Leela Visaria
   Gujarat Institute of Development
   Research (GIDR)
   Ahmedabad
8. Mr Subash Mendhapurkar
   Director
   Society for Uplift through
   Rural Action (SUTRA)
   Himachal Pradesh
9. Dr Nerges Mistry
   Senior Research Officer
   FRCH
   Mumbai
10. Ms Poonam Muthreja
    Country Coordinator
    MacArthur Foundation
    New Delhi
11. Dr Gyanendra Kumar
    Population Education Officer
    Family Planning Association of
    India (FPAI)
    New Delhi
12. Dr K.S. Krishnaswamy
    14th Main at 30th Cross
    Bangalore
13. Dr D. Banerji
    B-43, Panchsheel Enclave
    New Delhi
14. Dr Abusaleh Shariff
    Associate Director
    National Council of Applied
    Economic Research (NCAER)
    New Delhi
15. Ms Ratna Sudarshan
    NCAER
    New Delhi
16. Mr B.L. Joshi
    NCAER
    New Delhi
17. Ms. D.V. Rukmini
    NCAER
    New Delhi
18. Dr Shanti Ghosh
    5, Sri Aurobindo Marg
    New Delhi
19. Dr Manjula Chakravarty
    Deputy Advisor
    Planning Commission
20. Ms Devaki Jain
    Trustee and Ex-Director
    ISST
    New Delhi
21. Prof A. Vaidyanathan
    Trustee
    ISST
22. Dr Saraswathy Ganapathy
    14/33, 2nd Main Road, 8th Block
    Bangalore

23. Ms Claire Noronha
    Consultant
    ISST

24. Ms Kalpana Jain
    Journalist
    The Times of India
    New Delhi

PARTICIPANTS FROM ISST

1. Prof. Swapna Mukhopadhyay
2. Ms Praachi Tewari Gandhi
3. Ms R. Savithri
4. Ms Surekha Garimella
5. Ms Manjushree Mishra
6. Dr Rina Bhattacharya
7. Ms Pallavi Ghosh
8. Ms Raj Virdi
9. Ms Seema Sharma

Contributors

N.H. Antia	Director and Trustee of the Foundation for Research in Community Health, Mumbai.
S.N. Chaudhuri	Director, Child In Need Institute, Calcutta.
Ravi Duggal	Consultant, Centre for Health and Allied Themes, Mumbai.
Praachi Tewari Gandhi	Researcher, Institute of Social Studies Trust, New Delhi.
Surekha Garimella	Researcher, Institute of Social Studies Trust, New Delhi.
A.K. Shiv Kumar	Consultant, UNICEF, New Delhi.
Nerges Mistry	Senior Research Officer, the Foundation for Research in Community Health, Mumbai.
Swapna Mukhopadhyay	Director, Institute of Social Studies Trust, New Delhi.
Mohan Rao	Assistant Professor, School of Social Sciences, JNU, New Delhi.
T.K. Sundari Ravindran	Researcher and Founder member of Rural Women's Social Education Centre, Chengalpattu, Tamil Nadu.
R. Savithri	Researcher, Institute of Social Studies Trust, New Delhi.
Krishna Soman	Consultant, Institute of Social Studies Trust, New Delhi.

Index

Acquired Immuno Deficiency Syndrome (AIDS) 32, 42, 159, 160
adult education programme 138, 139
All India Institute of Hygiene and Public Health 56
Allen, B.C. 61
Alma Ata declaration 156-7, 181
anaemia 32, 33, 39
Anaemia Prophylaxis programme 33, 169
Andhra Pradesh 164
anganwadi workers 16, 17, 33
Antia, N.H. 18, 125-30, 167, 171, 172, 176, 177, 179
auxiliary nurse midwives (ANMs) 16, 17, 30, 33, 39, 114, 126, 133, 135, 153, 179
Ayurveda 38

Banerji, D. 168, 179
Beijing Conference 37
Bengal Famine 56
Beveridge Committee 151
bhagats 38
Bhore Committee 12, 23, 24, 25, 29, 35, 151, 152, 153, 168, 171, 180, 182
Bihar 54, 58, 59, 63, 64, 170

Cairo document 11, 12; and the role of the Clinton administration 11 *see also* International Conference on Population and Development
Calcutta 131, 168, 178
Centre for Enquiry into Health and Allied Themes (CEHAT) 167, 168
Chaddha Committee 153; report of 30
Chaudhuri, S.N. 18, 131-7, 168, 176, 178
Chengalpattu 138, 145, 176, 177

Child in Need Institute (CINI) 131-7, 168, 176, 178
CINI Nutrition Rehabilitation Centre (NRC) 131
Child Survival and Safe Motherhood (CSSM) 135
China 54, 170
Clinic Approach 152, 153
Committee on Multipurpose Workers 31, 155
Community Development Programme 152
Community health centres (CHCs) 159
Community Health Volunteers (CHV) Scheme 156, 157, 158
community health workers 16, 177
contraception, perceptions on 98; use of 71, 72, 73, 75, 80-9 *passim*, 94, 95, 99, 100, 102, 103, 116, 120, 140, 172, 173, 174; women's views on 107-9
contraceptive prevalence rate (CPR) 80
contraceptives, hazardous 37
Cuba 170

dai training programme 31
dais 24, 38, 39, 107, 131, 133, 178
Declaration of the International Decade for Women 29
Delhi 14, 104-20 *passim*, 174, 175
diaphragm 146
Duggal, R. 16, 37-52, 167, 168, 169, 170, 171

Emergency 13, 156, 181
England 51
Europe 152
Expanded Programme of Immunization 157

Expert Group on Population Policy 160
Extension Education Approach 153

Factory Act of 1934 24
Family Health Survey (FHS) 101
family planning programme 11, 13, 14, 25, 26, 30, 46, 103, 108, 152, 153, 154, 156, 159, 160, 180, 181; hierarchical and insensitive nature of the 12; and its link with women's health 11, 12
female sterilization 13, 39, 40, 46, 74, 95, 108, 142, 175
fertility behaviour 71, 73, 89, 92, 93, 94, 99, 174
fertility control programmes 11
Foundation for Research in Community Health (FRCH) 43, 127, 167, 176
Freire, P. 138

Ganapathy, S. 167, 176
Garimella, S. 14, 98-121, 172
gender inequality 14, 38, 53, 54, 66, 71, 72, 73, 75, 80, 88, 94, 99, 100, 134, 140, 170, 172
Gender-related Development Index (GDI) 54, 56, 58, 64, 170
Ghose, S. 168, 171, 172, 179
Gorakhpur 155
Gramin Uthan Samiti 106
Growth Monitoring, Oral Rehydration, Breast Feeding and Immunization (GOBI) 159

Haryana 56, 66
Health and Family Welfare, investment in 25
Health Survey and Planning Committee 30, 152
herbalists 38
Himachal Pradesh 56, 168, 171, 172
Homeopathy 38
Human Development Index (HDI) 54, 56, 57, 58, 170

Human Development Reports (HDRs) 53, 54

Indian Council of Medical Research (ICMR) 33, 34, 157, 177
Indian Council of Social Science Research (ICSSR) 34, 157
induced abortions 113-16
infant mortality rate (IMR) 58, 74, 161, 170
infertility 100, 103, 107
Integrated Child Development Services (ICDS) 33, 135, 182
International Conference on Population and Development (ICPD) 11, 14, 15, 37 *see also* Cairo document
Intra Uterine Contraceptive Device (IUCD) 39, 46, 108, 153, 154
invasive contraceptive technology 13

Johnston, A.M. 75

Kapkot 106
Karnataka 78, 164, 172
Kartar Singh Committee *see* Committee on Multipurpose Workers
Kasauni 106
Kerala 54, 56, 58-66, 72, 154, 161, 170
Kondhwa Leprosy Hospital 125
Konkan 126
Kumaon 14, 104, 106, 107, 110, 111, 113, 114, 115, 174, 175
Kumar, A.K. Shiva 53-68, 167, 168, 170
Krishnaji, N. 96
Krishnaswamy, K.S. 168, 179, 181-2, 183
Kynch, J. 63

Lakshmi Ashram 106
leprosarium 126
local disease/technique specialists 38
Ludhiana 63

MacArthur Foundation 128, 167
Madhya Pradesh 58, 161

INDEX

Madras 146
Maharashtra 56, 164
mahila mandals 131, 132, 178, 180
Mahmud, S. 75
Malaria Control Programme 29, 152
male sterilization 89, 117, 154, 155, 174
Malshiras 127
Manipur 54, 58-66, 170
marup 61
maternal and child health (MCH) programme 13, 14, 16, 23, 24, 25, 26, 29, 30, 31, 32, 34, 37, 39, 40, 46, 127, 131, 135, 152, 153, 156, 159, 168, 169, 179
maternal mortality rate (MMR) 24, 32, 169
Maternity Benefit Act 24
Mendhapurkar, S. 168, 171, 172
Miller, B. 74
Minimum Needs Programme (MNP) 31, 155, 156, 158
Ministry of Health and Family Welfare 14, 17
Mistry, N. 18, 125-30, 167, 176, 177
Mudaliar Committee *see* Health Survey and Planning Committee
Mukherji Committee 154; report of the 153
Mukhopadhyay, S. 14, 71-97, 98-121, 167, 171, 172, 176, 179, 183
multipurpose workers (MPWs) 16, 30, 31, 32, 135, 155, 157

Nairobi UN Conference 37
National Adult Education Programme (NAEP) 138
National AIDS Control Organization (NACO) 158
National AIDS Control Programme 158
National Council of Applied Economic Research (NCAER) 43, 44
National Disease Control Programmes 127

National Family Health Survey (NFHS) 40, 56, 59
National Health and Development Committee *see* Bhore Committee
National Health Service of England 151
National Institute of Health and Family Weflare (NIHFW) 43
National Institute of Public Finance and Policy (NIPFP) 44
National Malaria Eradication Programme (NMEP) 152, 153, 154, 156
National Planning Committee *see* Sokhey Committee
National Population Policy 17, 26, 156, 159
National Sample Survey (NSS) 40, 43
National Smallpox Eradication Programme (NSEP) 153, 154, 180
National Tuberculosis Programme (NTP) 153, 159, 160, 180
Nayak Committee 176
new economic policy 47
non-government organizations (NGOs) 12, 17-18, 23, 34, 39, 105, 106, 127, 130, 134, 135, 136, 142, 144, 145, 158, 167, 174, 179
numi 63
Nupi Lan (Women's War) 62

oral rehydration therapy (ORT) 143
Orissa 170

Panchayati Raj 34, 128, 129, 179, 180
paramedics 38, 39
Parinche 128, 177
patriarchal values 14
Population Council 155
primary health care (PHC) 16, 27, 29, 30, 31, 32, 33, 34, 37, 38, 40, 46, 47, 48, 74, 105, 106, 114, 126, 127, 134, 135, 141, 143, 146, 152, 153, 157, 159, 165, 169, 179, 180, 181
private health services 38, 39, 40, 44, 47, 49, 50, 51, 126, 169

public health nurses (PHN) 24, 29, 135
public health programmes, neglect of 25
public health services 38, 39, 40, 45, 47, 48, 49, 50, 52, 126, 127, 169, 183
puerperal sepsis 32, 33
Punjab 56, 66, 170

Rajasthan 58, 59, 63, 161, 170
Rao, M. 16, 151-66, 167, 168, 180-1, 183
Ravindran, T.K.S. 18, 73, 138-48, 167, 176, 177, 178, 179
Reinforced Programme 153
Reorganized Programme 153
reproductive behaviour *see* fertility behaviour
reproductive choice 15, 71, 72, 73, 74, 75, 86, 88, 94, 98, 99, 100, 101, 103, 104, 172, 173, 174
reproductive child health (RCH) 14, 17
reproductive tract infections (RTI) 132, 140, 143
ROME scheme 157
Rukmini, D.V. 176
Rural Women's Social Education Centre (RUWSEC) 138-48, 167, 177, 179

Sachar, R.K. 63
Sahabhagi Gramin Vikas 106
Sample Registration System (SRS) 92
Savithri, R. 14, 71-97, 172
Selective Primary Health Care Approach 157
Sen, A. 57, 63
sexually transmitted diseases (STD) 132, 143, 178, 179, 182
Shrivastava Committee 156, 181
Siddha 38
Singh, J.N. 62
Singrur 56
Society for Uplift through Rural Action (SUTRA) 168
Sokhey Committee 23, 24, 32, 168
Soman, K. 13, 23-36, 167, 168, 169
Soviet Union 151

Sri Lanka 170
structural adjustment programmes, and the impact on public health sector 16, 47, 160

Tamil Nadu 138, 140, 145, 164, 167, 176, 177
target-free approach in family welfare 14
targeted population control programmes, failure of 12
Tewari Gandhi, P. 14, 71-97, 172
total fertility rate (TFR) 57, 58
tubectomy *see* female sterilization
Tuberculosis Control Programme 29, 46

Unani 38
unipurpose workers 25, 32
United Nations Advisory Mission 30, 153
United Nations Children's Educational Fund (UNICEF) 27, 156, 167, 168
United Nations Development Programme (UNDP) 53, 54
Universal Immunization Programme (UIP) 158, 159
User's Perspective Studies on Norplant Acceptors 146
Uttar Pradesh 14, 54, 58, 59, 64, 71, 72, 78, 92, 95, 106, 161, 170, 171, 172

vasectomy *see* male sterilization
village health workers 16, 33, 114
voodoos 38

West Bengal 133
witch doctors 38
Women's Health Movement 12, 14
Working Group on Population Policy 26, 27, 157, 158
World Bank 155, 158, 160, 182
World Fertility Survey 75
World Health Organization (WHO) 50, 51, 156, 157, 158
World Population Conference 26